C-100　　CAREER EXAMINATION SERIES

*This is your
PASSBOOK for...*

Bus Maintainer, Group A

*Test Preparation Study Guide
Questions & Answers*

COPYRIGHT NOTICE

This book is SOLELY intended for, is sold ONLY to, and its use is RESTRICTED to individual, bona fide applicants or candidates who qualify by virtue of having seriously filed applications for appropriate license, certificate, professional and/or promotional advancement, higher school matriculation, scholarship, or other legitimate requirements of education and/or governmental authorities.

This book is NOT intended for use, class instruction, tutoring, training, duplication, copying, reprinting, excerption, or adaptation, etc., by:

1) Other publishers
2) Proprietors and/or Instructors of "Coaching" and/or Preparatory Courses
3) Personnel and/or Training Divisions of commercial, industrial, and governmental organizations
4) Schools, colleges, or universities and/or their departments and staffs, including teachers and other personnel
5) Testing Agencies or Bureaus
6) Study groups which seek by the purchase of a single volume to copy and/or duplicate and/or adapt this material for use by the group as a whole without having purchased individual volumes for each of the members of the group
7) Et al.

Such persons would be in violation of appropriate Federal and State statutes.

PROVISION OF LICENSING AGREEMENTS – Recognized educational, commercial, industrial, and governmental institutions and organizations, and others legitimately engaged in educational pursuits, including training, testing, and measurement activities, may address request for a licensing agreement to the copyright owners, who will determine whether, and under what conditions, including fees and charges, the materials in this book may be used them. In other words, a licensing facility exists for the legitimate use of the material in this book on other than an individual basis. However, it is asseverated and affirmed here that the material in this book CANNOT be used without the receipt of the express permission of such a licensing agreement from the Publishers. Inquiries re licensing should be addressed to the company, attention rights and permissions department.

All rights reserved, including the right of reproduction in whole or in part, in any form or by any means, electronic or mechanical, including photocopying, recording, or by any information storage and retrieval system, without permission in writing from the Publisher.

Copyright © 2024 by
National Learning Corporation

212 Michael Drive, Syosset, NY 11791
(516) 921-8888 • www.passbooks.com
E-mail: info@passbooks.com

PUBLISHED IN THE UNITED STATES OF AMERICA

PASSBOOK® SERIES

THE *PASSBOOK® SERIES* has been created to prepare applicants and candidates for the ultimate academic battlefield – the examination room.

At some time in our lives, each and every one of us may be required to take an examination – for validation, matriculation, admission, qualification, registration, certification, or licensure.

Based on the assumption that every applicant or candidate has met the basic formal educational standards, has taken the required number of courses, and read the necessary texts, the *PASSBOOK® SERIES* furnishes the one special preparation which may assure passing with confidence, instead of failing with insecurity. Examination questions – together with answers – are furnished as the basic vehicle for study so that the mysteries of the examination and its compounding difficulties may be eliminated or diminished by a sure method.

This book is meant to help you pass your examination provided that you qualify and are serious in your objective.

The entire field is reviewed through the huge store of content information which is succinctly presented through a provocative and challenging approach – the question-and-answer method.

A climate of success is established by furnishing the correct answers at the end of each test.

You soon learn to recognize types of questions, forms of questions, and patterns of questioning. You may even begin to anticipate expected outcomes.

You perceive that many questions are repeated or adapted so that you can gain acute insights, which may enable you to score many sure points.

You learn how to confront new questions, or types of questions, and to attack them confidently and work out the correct answers.

You note objectives and emphases, and recognize pitfalls and dangers, so that you may make positive educational adjustments.

Moreover, you are kept fully informed in relation to new concepts, methods, practices, and directions in the field.

You discover that you are actually taking the examination all the time: you are preparing for the examination by "taking" an examination, not by reading extraneous and/or supererogatory textbooks.

In short, this PASSBOOK®, used directedly, should be an important factor in helping you to pass your test.

BUS MAINTAINER, GROUP A

DUTIES:

Bus Maintainers, Group A, under supervision, maintain, install, inspect, test, alter and repair the bodies and related mechanical, structural, and electrical equipment of buses and other automotive vehicles, including servicing, repairing and installing doors, seats, windows, framing, sheeting, hand bars, signs, floors, radiators, heat exchangers, bumpers, light fixtures and headlights; make and repair sheet metal or fiberglass body sections and structural members of buses using such tools and machines as are necessary; weld bus bodies and parts; disassemble bus bodies and parts using burning equipment; prepare vehicle bodies for painting; sand as necessary; spray and brush paint bus, truck and automobile bodies; manually and electronically document work activities; read and interpret technical documents, diagrams, and schematics; drive motor vehicles and operate machinery; and perform related work.

THE TEST

The test will measure your ability to maintain and repair bodies, undercarriages, and associated components of buses, automobiles, and trucks, and may include: body sheeting repair, preparation, and painting; the proper use and selection of tools, machinery, and materials; fabrication and welding; reading and interpreting specifications and drawings; relevant mathematical calculations; and other related areas.

HOW TO TAKE A TEST

I. YOU MUST PASS AN EXAMINATION

A. *WHAT EVERY CANDIDATE SHOULD KNOW*

Examination applicants often ask us for help in preparing for the written test. What can I study in advance? What kinds of questions will be asked? How will the test be given? How will the papers be graded?

As an applicant for a civil service examination, you may be wondering about some of these things. Our purpose here is to suggest effective methods of advance study and to describe civil service examinations.

Your chances for success on this examination can be increased if you know how to prepare. Those "pre-examination jitters" can be reduced if you know what to expect. You can even experience an adventure in good citizenship if you know why civil service exams are given.

B. *WHY ARE CIVIL SERVICE EXAMINATIONS GIVEN?*

Civil service examinations are important to you in two ways. As a citizen, you want public jobs filled by employees who know how to do their work. As a job seeker, you want a fair chance to compete for that job on an equal footing with other candidates. The best-known means of accomplishing this two-fold goal is the competitive examination.

Exams are widely publicized throughout the nation. They may be administered for jobs in federal, state, city, municipal, town or village governments or agencies.

Any citizen may apply, with some limitations, such as the age or residence of applicants. Your experience and education may be reviewed to see whether you meet the requirements for the particular examination. When these requirements exist, they are reasonable and applied consistently to all applicants. Thus, a competitive examination may cause you some uneasiness now, but it is your privilege and safeguard.

C. *HOW ARE CIVIL SERVICE EXAMS DEVELOPED?*

Examinations are carefully written by trained technicians who are specialists in the field known as "psychological measurement," in consultation with recognized authorities in the field of work that the test will cover. These experts recommend the subject matter areas or skills to be tested; only those knowledges or skills important to your success on the job are included. The most reliable books and source materials available are used as references. Together, the experts and technicians judge the difficulty level of the questions.

Test technicians know how to phrase questions so that the problem is clearly stated. Their ethics do not permit "trick" or "catch" questions. Questions may have been tried out on sample groups, or subjected to statistical analysis, to determine their usefulness.

Written tests are often used in combination with performance tests, ratings of training and experience, and oral interviews. All of these measures combine to form the best-known means of finding the right person for the right job.

II. HOW TO PASS THE WRITTEN TEST

A. NATURE OF THE EXAMINATION

To prepare intelligently for civil service examinations, you should know how they differ from school examinations you have taken. In school you were assigned certain definite pages to read or subjects to cover. The examination questions were quite detailed and usually emphasized memory. Civil service exams, on the other hand, try to discover your present ability to perform the duties of a position, plus your potentiality to learn these duties. In other words, a civil service exam attempts to predict how successful you will be. Questions cover such a broad area that they cannot be as minute and detailed as school exam questions.

In the public service similar kinds of work, or positions, are grouped together in one "class." This process is known as *position-classification*. All the positions in a class are paid according to the salary range for that class. One class title covers all of these positions, and they are all tested by the same examination.

B. FOUR BASIC STEPS

1) Study the announcement

How, then, can you know what subjects to study? Our best answer is: "Learn as much as possible about the class of positions for which you've applied." The exam will test the knowledge, skills and abilities needed to do the work.

Your most valuable source of information about the position you want is the official exam announcement. This announcement lists the training and experience qualifications. Check these standards and apply only if you come reasonably close to meeting them.

The brief description of the position in the examination announcement offers some clues to the subjects which will be tested. Think about the job itself. Review the duties in your mind. Can you perform them, or are there some in which you are rusty? Fill in the blank spots in your preparation.

Many jurisdictions preview the written test in the exam announcement by including a section called "Knowledge and Abilities Required," "Scope of the Examination," or some similar heading. Here you will find out specifically what fields will be tested.

2) Review your own background

Once you learn in general what the position is all about, and what you need to know to do the work, ask yourself which subjects you already know fairly well and which need improvement. You may wonder whether to concentrate on improving your strong areas or on building some background in your fields of weakness. When the announcement has specified "some knowledge" or "considerable knowledge," or has used adjectives like "beginning principles of…" or "advanced … methods," you can get a clue as to the number and difficulty of questions to be asked in any given field. More questions, and hence broader coverage, would be included for those subjects which are more important in the work. Now weigh your strengths and weaknesses against the job requirements and prepare accordingly.

3) Determine the level of the position

Another way to tell how intensively you should prepare is to understand the level of the job for which you are applying. Is it the entering level? In other words, is this the position in which beginners in a field of work are hired? Or is it an intermediate or advanced level? Sometimes this is indicated by such words as "Junior" or "Senior" in the class title. Other jurisdictions use Roman numerals to designate the level – Clerk I, Clerk II, for example. The word "Supervisor" sometimes appears in the title. If the level is not indicated by the title, check the description of duties. Will you be working under very close supervision, or will you have responsibility for independent decisions in this work?

4) Choose appropriate study materials

Now that you know the subjects to be examined and the relative amount of each subject to be covered, you can choose suitable study materials. For beginning level jobs, or even advanced ones, if you have a pronounced weakness in some aspect of your training, read a modern, standard textbook in that field. Be sure it is up to date and has general coverage. Such books are normally available at your library, and the librarian will be glad to help you locate one. For entry-level positions, questions of appropriate difficulty are chosen – neither highly advanced questions, nor those too simple. Such questions require careful thought but not advanced training.

If the position for which you are applying is technical or advanced, you will read more advanced, specialized material. If you are already familiar with the basic principles of your field, elementary textbooks would waste your time. Concentrate on advanced textbooks and technical periodicals. Think through the concepts and review difficult problems in your field.

These are all general sources. You can get more ideas on your own initiative, following these leads. For example, training manuals and publications of the government agency which employs workers in your field can be useful, particularly for technical and professional positions. A letter or visit to the government department involved may result in more specific study suggestions, and certainly will provide you with a more definite idea of the exact nature of the position you are seeking.

III. KINDS OF TESTS

Tests are used for purposes other than measuring knowledge and ability to perform specified duties. For some positions, it is equally important to test ability to make adjustments to new situations or to profit from training. In others, basic mental abilities not dependent on information are essential. Questions which test these things may not appear as pertinent to the duties of the position as those which test for knowledge and information. Yet they are often highly important parts of a fair examination. For very general questions, it is almost impossible to help you direct your study efforts. What we can do is to point out some of the more common of these general abilities needed in public service positions and describe some typical questions.

1) General information

Broad, general information has been found useful for predicting job success in some kinds of work. This is tested in a variety of ways, from vocabulary lists to questions about current events. Basic background in some field of work, such as sociology or economics, may be sampled in a group of questions. Often these are principles which have become familiar to most persons through exposure rather than through formal training. It is difficult to advise you how to study for these questions; being alert to the world around you is our best suggestion.

2) Verbal ability

An example of an ability needed in many positions is verbal or language ability. Verbal ability is, in brief, the ability to use and understand words. Vocabulary and grammar tests are typical measures of this ability. Reading comprehension or paragraph interpretation questions are common in many kinds of civil service tests. You are given a paragraph of written material and asked to find its central meaning.

3) Numerical ability

Number skills can be tested by the familiar arithmetic problem, by checking paired lists of numbers to see which are alike and which are different, or by interpreting charts and graphs. In the latter test, a graph may be printed in the test booklet which you are asked to use as the basis for answering questions.

4) Observation

A popular test for law-enforcement positions is the observation test. A picture is shown to you for several minutes, then taken away. Questions about the picture test your ability to observe both details and larger elements.

5) Following directions

In many positions in the public service, the employee must be able to carry out written instructions dependably and accurately. You may be given a chart with several columns, each column listing a variety of information. The questions require you to carry out directions involving the information given in the chart.

6) Skills and aptitudes

Performance tests effectively measure some manual skills and aptitudes. When the skill is one in which you are trained, such as typing or shorthand, you can practice. These tests are often very much like those given in business school or high school courses. For many of the other skills and aptitudes, however, no short-time preparation can be made. Skills and abilities natural to you or that you have developed throughout your lifetime are being tested.

Many of the general questions just described provide all the data needed to answer the questions and ask you to use your reasoning ability to find the answers. Your best preparation for these tests, as well as for tests of facts and ideas, is to be at your physical and mental best. You, no doubt, have your own methods of getting into an exam-taking mood and keeping "in shape." The next section lists some ideas on this subject.

IV. KINDS OF QUESTIONS

Only rarely is the "essay" question, which you answer in narrative form, used in civil service tests. Civil service tests are usually of the short-answer type. Full instructions for answering these questions will be given to you at the examination. But in case this is your first experience with short-answer questions and separate answer sheets, here is what you need to know:

1) Multiple-choice Questions

Most popular of the short-answer questions is the "multiple choice" or "best answer" question. It can be used, for example, to test for factual knowledge, ability to solve problems or judgment in meeting situations found at work.

A multiple-choice question is normally one of three types—
- It can begin with an incomplete statement followed by several possible endings. You are to find the one ending which *best* completes the statement, although some of the others may not be entirely wrong.
- It can also be a complete statement in the form of a question which is answered by choosing one of the statements listed.

- It can be in the form of a problem – again you select the best answer.

Here is an example of a multiple-choice question with a discussion which should give you some clues as to the method for choosing the right answer:

When an employee has a complaint about his assignment, the action which will *best* help him overcome his difficulty is to
- A. discuss his difficulty with his coworkers
- B. take the problem to the head of the organization
- C. take the problem to the person who gave him the assignment
- D. say nothing to anyone about his complaint

In answering this question, you should study each of the choices to find which is best. Consider choice "A" – Certainly an employee may discuss his complaint with fellow employees, but no change or improvement can result, and the complaint remains unresolved. Choice "B" is a poor choice since the head of the organization probably does not know what assignment you have been given, and taking your problem to him is known as "going over the head" of the supervisor. The supervisor, or person who made the assignment, is the person who can clarify it or correct any injustice. Choice "C" is, therefore, correct. To say nothing, as in choice "D," is unwise. Supervisors have and interest in knowing the problems employees are facing, and the employee is seeking a solution to his problem.

2) True/False Questions

The "true/false" or "right/wrong" form of question is sometimes used. Here a complete statement is given. Your job is to decide whether the statement is right or wrong.

SAMPLE: A roaming cell-phone call to a nearby city costs less than a non-roaming call to a distant city.

This statement is wrong, or false, since roaming calls are more expensive.

This is not a complete list of all possible question forms, although most of the others are variations of these common types. You will always get complete directions for answering questions. Be sure you understand *how* to mark your answers – ask questions until you do.

V. RECORDING YOUR ANSWERS

Computer terminals are used more and more today for many different kinds of exams.

For an examination with very few applicants, you may be told to record your answers in the test booklet itself. Separate answer sheets are much more common. If this separate answer sheet is to be scored by machine – and this is often the case – it is highly important that you mark your answers correctly in order to get credit.

An electronic scoring machine is often used in civil service offices because of the speed with which papers can be scored. Machine-scored answer sheets must be marked with a pencil, which will be given to you. This pencil has a high graphite content which responds to the electronic scoring machine. As a matter of fact, stray dots may register as answers, so do not let your pencil rest on the answer sheet while you are pondering the correct answer. Also, if your pencil lead breaks or is otherwise defective, ask for another.

Since the answer sheet will be dropped in a slot in the scoring machine, be careful not to bend the corners or get the paper crumpled.

The answer sheet normally has five vertical columns of numbers, with 30 numbers to a column. These numbers correspond to the question numbers in your test booklet. After each number, going across the page are four or five pairs of dotted lines. These short dotted lines have small letters or numbers above them. The first two pairs may also have a "T" or "F" above the letters. This indicates that the first two pairs only are to be used if the questions are of the true-false type. If the questions are multiple choice, disregard the "T" and "F" and pay attention only to the small letters or numbers.

Answer your questions in the manner of the sample that follows:

32. The largest city in the United States is
    A. Washington, D.C.
    B. New York City
    C. Chicago
    D. Detroit
    E. San Francisco

1) Choose the answer you think is best. (New York City is the largest, so "B" is correct.)
2) Find the row of dotted lines numbered the same as the question you are answering. (Find row number 32)
3) Find the pair of dotted lines corresponding to the answer. (Find the pair of lines under the mark "B.")
4) Make a solid black mark between the dotted lines.

VI. BEFORE THE TEST

Common sense will help you find procedures to follow to get ready for an examination. Too many of us, however, overlook these sensible measures. Indeed, nervousness and fatigue have been found to be the most serious reasons why applicants fail to do their best on civil service tests. Here is a list of reminders:

- Begin your preparation early – Don't wait until the last minute to go scurrying around for books and materials or to find out what the position is all about.
- Prepare continuously – An hour a night for a week is better than an all-night cram session. This has been definitely established. What is more, a night a week for a month will return better dividends than crowding your study into a shorter period of time.
- Locate the place of the exam – You have been sent a notice telling you when and where to report for the examination. If the location is in a different town or otherwise unfamiliar to you, it would be well to inquire the best route and learn something about the building.
- Relax the night before the test – Allow your mind to rest. Do not study at all that night. Plan some mild recreation or diversion; then go to bed early and get a good night's sleep.
- Get up early enough to make a leisurely trip to the place for the test – This way unforeseen events, traffic snarls, unfamiliar buildings, etc. will not upset you.
- Dress comfortably – A written test is not a fashion show. You will be known by number and not by name, so wear something comfortable.

- Leave excess paraphernalia at home – Shopping bags and odd bundles will get in your way. You need bring only the items mentioned in the official notice you received; usually everything you need is provided. Do not bring reference books to the exam. They will only confuse those last minutes and be taken away from you when in the test room.
- Arrive somewhat ahead of time – If because of transportation schedules you must get there very early, bring a newspaper or magazine to take your mind off yourself while waiting.
- Locate the examination room – When you have found the proper room, you will be directed to the seat or part of the room where you will sit. Sometimes you are given a sheet of instructions to read while you are waiting. Do not fill out any forms until you are told to do so; just read them and be prepared.
- Relax and prepare to listen to the instructions
- If you have any physical problem that may keep you from doing your best, be sure to tell the test administrator. If you are sick or in poor health, you really cannot do your best on the exam. You can come back and take the test some other time.

VII. AT THE TEST

The day of the test is here and you have the test booklet in your hand. The temptation to get going is very strong. Caution! There is more to success than knowing the right answers. You must know how to identify your papers and understand variations in the type of short-answer question used in this particular examination. Follow these suggestions for maximum results from your efforts:

1) Cooperate with the monitor

The test administrator has a duty to create a situation in which you can be as much at ease as possible. He will give instructions, tell you when to begin, check to see that you are marking your answer sheet correctly, and so on. He is not there to guard you, although he will see that your competitors do not take unfair advantage. He wants to help you do your best.

2) Listen to all instructions

Don't jump the gun! Wait until you understand all directions. In most civil service tests you get more time than you need to answer the questions. So don't be in a hurry. Read each word of instructions until you clearly understand the meaning. Study the examples, listen to all announcements and follow directions. Ask questions if you do not understand what to do.

3) Identify your papers

Civil service exams are usually identified by number only. You will be assigned a number; you must not put your name on your test papers. Be sure to copy your number correctly. Since more than one exam may be given, copy your exact examination title.

4) Plan your time

Unless you are told that a test is a "speed" or "rate of work" test, speed itself is usually not important. Time enough to answer all the questions will be provided, but this does not mean that you have all day. An overall time limit has been set. Divide the total time (in minutes) by the number of questions to determine the approximate time you have for each question.

5) Do not linger over difficult questions

If you come across a difficult question, mark it with a paper clip (useful to have along) and come back to it when you have been through the booklet. One caution if you do this – be sure to skip a number on your answer sheet as well. Check often to be sure that you have not lost your place and that you are marking in the row numbered the same as the question you are answering.

6) Read the questions

Be sure you know what the question asks! Many capable people are unsuccessful because they failed to *read* the questions correctly.

7) Answer all questions

Unless you have been instructed that a penalty will be deducted for incorrect answers, it is better to guess than to omit a question.

8) Speed tests

It is often better NOT to guess on speed tests. It has been found that on timed tests people are tempted to spend the last few seconds before time is called in marking answers at random – without even reading them – in the hope of picking up a few extra points. To discourage this practice, the instructions may warn you that your score will be "corrected" for guessing. That is, a penalty will be applied. The incorrect answers will be deducted from the correct ones, or some other penalty formula will be used.

9) Review your answers

If you finish before time is called, go back to the questions you guessed or omitted to give them further thought. Review other answers if you have time.

10) Return your test materials

If you are ready to leave before others have finished or time is called, take ALL your materials to the monitor and leave quietly. Never take any test material with you. The monitor can discover whose papers are not complete, and taking a test booklet may be grounds for disqualification.

VIII. EXAMINATION TECHNIQUES

1) Read the general instructions carefully. These are usually printed on the first page of the exam booklet. As a rule, these instructions refer to the timing of the examination; the fact that you should not start work until the signal and must stop work at a signal, etc. If there are any *special* instructions, such as a choice of questions to be answered, make sure that you note this instruction carefully.

2) When you are ready to start work on the examination, that is as soon as the signal has been given, read the instructions to each question booklet, underline any key words or phrases, such as *least, best, outline, describe* and the like. In this way you will tend to answer as requested rather than discover on reviewing your paper that you *listed without describing*, that you selected the *worst* choice rather than the *best* choice, etc.

3) If the examination is of the objective or multiple-choice type – that is, each question will also give a series of possible answers: A, B, C or D, and you are called upon to select the best answer and write the letter next to that answer on your answer paper – it is advisable to start answering each question in turn. There may be anywhere from 50 to 100 such questions in the three or four hours allotted and you can see how much time would be taken if you read through all the questions before beginning to answer any. Furthermore, if you come across a question or group of questions which you know would be difficult to answer, it would undoubtedly affect your handling of all the other questions.

4) If the examination is of the essay type and contains but a few questions, it is a moot point as to whether you should read all the questions before starting to answer any one. Of course, if you are given a choice – say five out of seven and the like – then it is essential to read all the questions so you can eliminate the two that are most difficult. If, however, you are asked to answer all the questions, there may be danger in trying to answer the easiest one first because you may find that you will spend too much time on it. The best technique is to answer the first question, then proceed to the second, etc.

5) Time your answers. Before the exam begins, write down the time it started, then add the time allowed for the examination and write down the time it must be completed, then divide the time available somewhat as follows:
    - If 3-1/2 hours are allowed, that would be 210 minutes. If you have 80 objective-type questions, that would be an average of 2-1/2 minutes per question. Allow yourself no more than 2 minutes per question, or a total of 160 minutes, which will permit about 50 minutes to review.
    - If for the time allotment of 210 minutes there are 7 essay questions to answer, that would average about 30 minutes a question. Give yourself only 25 minutes per question so that you have about 35 minutes to review.

6) The most important instruction is to *read each question* and make sure you know what is wanted. The second most important instruction is to *time yourself properly* so that you answer every question. The third most important instruction is to *answer every question*. Guess if you have to but include something for each question. Remember that you will receive no credit for a blank and will probably receive some credit if you write something in answer to an essay question. If you guess a letter – say "B" for a multiple-choice question – you may have guessed right. If you leave a blank as an answer to a multiple-choice question, the examiners may respect your feelings but it will not add a point to your score. Some exams may penalize you for wrong answers, so in such cases *only*, you may not want to guess unless you have some basis for your answer.

7) Suggestions
    a. Objective-type questions
        1. Examine the question booklet for proper sequence of pages and questions
        2. Read all instructions carefully
        3. Skip any question which seems too difficult; return to it after all other questions have been answered
        4. Apportion your time properly; do not spend too much time on any single question or group of questions

5. Note and underline key words – *all, most, fewest, least, best, worst, same, opposite*, etc.
6. Pay particular attention to negatives
7. Note unusual option, e.g., unduly long, short, complex, different or similar in content to the body of the question
8. Observe the use of "hedging" words – *probably, may, most likely*, etc.
9. Make sure that your answer is put next to the same number as the question
10. Do not second-guess unless you have good reason to believe the second answer is definitely more correct
11. Cross out original answer if you decide another answer is more accurate; do not erase until you are ready to hand your paper in
12. Answer all questions; guess unless instructed otherwise
13. Leave time for review

b. Essay questions
1. Read each question carefully
2. Determine exactly what is wanted. Underline key words or phrases.
3. Decide on outline or paragraph answer
4. Include many different points and elements unless asked to develop any one or two points or elements
5. Show impartiality by giving pros and cons unless directed to select one side only
6. Make and write down any assumptions you find necessary to answer the questions
7. Watch your English, grammar, punctuation and choice of words
8. Time your answers; don't crowd material

8) Answering the essay question

Most essay questions can be answered by framing the specific response around several key words or ideas. Here are a few such key words or ideas:

M's: manpower, materials, methods, money, management
P's: purpose, program, policy, plan, procedure, practice, problems, pitfalls, personnel, public relations
   a. Six basic steps in handling problems:
      1. Preliminary plan and background development
      2. Collect information, data and facts
      3. Analyze and interpret information, data and facts
      4. Analyze and develop solutions as well as make recommendations
      5. Prepare report and sell recommendations
      6. Install recommendations and follow up effectiveness

   b. Pitfalls to avoid
      1. *Taking things for granted* – A statement of the situation does not necessarily imply that each of the elements is necessarily true; for example, a complaint may be invalid and biased so that all that can be taken for granted is that a complaint has been registered

2. *Considering only one side of a situation* – Wherever possible, indicate several alternatives and then point out the reasons you selected the best one
3. *Failing to indicate follow up* – Whenever your answer indicates action on your part, make certain that you will take proper follow-up action to see how successful your recommendations, procedures or actions turn out to be
4. *Taking too long in answering any single question* – Remember to time your answers properly

IX. AFTER THE TEST

Scoring procedures differ in detail among civil service jurisdictions although the general principles are the same. Whether the papers are hand-scored or graded by machine we have described, they are nearly always graded by number. That is, the person who marks the paper knows only the number – never the name – of the applicant. Not until all the papers have been graded will they be matched with names. If other tests, such as training and experience or oral interview ratings have been given, scores will be combined. Different parts of the examination usually have different weights. For example, the written test might count 60 percent of the final grade, and a rating of training and experience 40 percent. In many jurisdictions, veterans will have a certain number of points added to their grades.

After the final grade has been determined, the names are placed in grade order and an eligible list is established. There are various methods for resolving ties between those who get the same final grade – probably the most common is to place first the name of the person whose application was received first. Job offers are made from the eligible list in the order the names appear on it. You will be notified of your grade and your rank as soon as all these computations have been made. This will be done as rapidly as possible.

People who are found to meet the requirements in the announcement are called "eligibles." Their names are put on a list of eligible candidates. An eligible's chances of getting a job depend on how high he stands on this list and how fast agencies are filling jobs from the list.

When a job is to be filled from a list of eligibles, the agency asks for the names of people on the list of eligibles for that job. When the civil service commission receives this request, it sends to the agency the names of the three people highest on this list. Or, if the job to be filled has specialized requirements, the office sends the agency the names of the top three persons who meet these requirements from the general list.

The appointing officer makes a choice from among the three people whose names were sent to him. If the selected person accepts the appointment, the names of the others are put back on the list to be considered for future openings.

That is the rule in hiring from all kinds of eligible lists, whether they are for typist, carpenter, chemist, or something else. For every vacancy, the appointing officer has his choice of any one of the top three eligibles on the list. This explains why the person whose name is on top of the list sometimes does not get an appointment when some of the persons lower on the list do. If the appointing officer chooses the second or third eligible, the No. 1 eligible does not get a job at once, but stays on the list until he is appointed or the list is terminated.

X. HOW TO PASS THE INTERVIEW TEST

The examination for which you applied requires an oral interview test. You have already taken the written test and you are now being called for the interview test – the final part of the formal examination.

You may think that it is not possible to prepare for an interview test and that there are no procedures to follow during an interview. Our purpose is to point out some things you can do in advance that will help you and some good rules to follow and pitfalls to avoid while you are being interviewed.

What is an interview supposed to test?

The written examination is designed to test the technical knowledge and competence of the candidate; the oral is designed to evaluate intangible qualities, not readily measured otherwise, and to establish a list showing the relative fitness of each candidate – as measured against his competitors – for the position sought. Scoring is not on the basis of "right" and "wrong," but on a sliding scale of values ranging from "not passable" to "outstanding." As a matter of fact, it is possible to achieve a relatively low score without a single "incorrect" answer because of evident weakness in the qualities being measured.

Occasionally, an examination may consist entirely of an oral test – either an individual or a group oral. In such cases, information is sought concerning the technical knowledges and abilities of the candidate, since there has been no written examination for this purpose. More commonly, however, an oral test is used to supplement a written examination.

Who conducts interviews?

The composition of oral boards varies among different jurisdictions. In nearly all, a representative of the personnel department serves as chairman. One of the members of the board may be a representative of the department in which the candidate would work. In some cases, "outside experts" are used, and, frequently, a businessman or some other representative of the general public is asked to serve. Labor and management or other special groups may be represented. The aim is to secure the services of experts in the appropriate field.

However the board is composed, it is a good idea (and not at all improper or unethical) to ascertain in advance of the interview who the members are and what groups they represent. When you are introduced to them, you will have some idea of their backgrounds and interests, and at least you will not stutter and stammer over their names.

What should be done before the interview?

While knowledge about the board members is useful and takes some of the surprise element out of the interview, there is other preparation which is more substantive. It *is* possible to prepare for an oral interview – in several ways:

1) Keep a copy of your application and review it carefully before the interview

This may be the only document before the oral board, and the starting point of the interview. Know what education and experience you have listed there, and the sequence and dates of all of it. Sometimes the board will ask you to review the highlights of your experience for them; you should not have to hem and haw doing it.

2) Study the class specification and the examination announcement

Usually, the oral board has one or both of these to guide them. The qualities, characteristics or knowledges required by the position sought are stated in these documents. They offer valuable clues as to the nature of the oral interview. For example, if the job involves supervisory responsibilities, the announcement will usually indicate that knowledge of modern supervisory methods and the qualifications of the candidate as a supervisor will be tested. If so, you can expect such questions, frequently in the form of a hypothetical situation which you are expected to solve. NEVER go into an oral without knowledge of the duties and responsibilities of the job you seek.

3) Think through each qualification required

Try to visualize the kind of questions you would ask if you were a board member. How well could you answer them? Try especially to appraise your own knowledge and background in each area, *measured against the job sought*, and identify any areas in which you are weak. Be critical and realistic – do not flatter yourself.

4) Do some general reading in areas in which you feel you may be weak

For example, if the job involves supervision and your past experience has NOT, some general reading in supervisory methods and practices, particularly in the field of human relations, might be useful. Do NOT study agency procedures or detailed manuals. The oral board will be testing your understanding and capacity, not your memory.

5) Get a good night's sleep and watch your general health and mental attitude

You will want a clear head at the interview. Take care of a cold or any other minor ailment, and of course, no hangovers.

What should be done on the day of the interview?

Now comes the day of the interview itself. Give yourself plenty of time to get there. Plan to arrive somewhat ahead of the scheduled time, particularly if your appointment is in the fore part of the day. If a previous candidate fails to appear, the board might be ready for you a bit early. By early afternoon an oral board is almost invariably behind schedule if there are many candidates, and you may have to wait. Take along a book or magazine to read, or your application to review, but leave any extraneous material in the waiting room when you go in for your interview. In any event, relax and compose yourself.

The matter of dress is important. The board is forming impressions about you – from your experience, your manners, your attitude, and your appearance. Give your personal appearance careful attention. Dress your best, but not your flashiest. Choose conservative, appropriate clothing, and be sure it is immaculate. This is a business interview, and your appearance should indicate that you regard it as such. Besides, being well groomed and properly dressed will help boost your confidence.

Sooner or later, someone will call your name and escort you into the interview room. *This is it.* From here on you are on your own. It is too late for any more preparation. But remember, you asked for this opportunity to prove your fitness, and you are here because your request was granted.

What happens when you go in?

The usual sequence of events will be as follows: The clerk (who is often the board stenographer) will introduce you to the chairman of the oral board, who will introduce you to the other members of the board. Acknowledge the introductions before you sit down. Do not be surprised if you find a microphone facing you or a stenotypist sitting by. Oral interviews are usually recorded in the event of an appeal or other review.

Usually the chairman of the board will open the interview by reviewing the highlights of your education and work experience from your application – primarily for the benefit of the other members of the board, as well as to get the material into the record. Do not interrupt or comment unless there is an error or significant misinterpretation; if that is the case, do not hesitate. But do not quibble about insignificant matters. Also, he will usually ask you some question about your education, experience or your present job – partly to get you to start talking and to establish the interviewing "rapport." He may start the actual questioning, or turn it over to one of the other members. Frequently, each member undertakes the questioning on a particular area, one in which he is perhaps most competent, so you can expect each member to participate in the examination. Because time is limited, you may also expect some rather abrupt switches in the direction the questioning takes, so do not be upset by it. Normally, a board member will not pursue a single line of questioning unless he discovers a particular strength or weakness.

After each member has participated, the chairman will usually ask whether any member has any further questions, then will ask you if you have anything you wish to add. Unless you are expecting this question, it may floor you. Worse, it may start you off on an extended, extemporaneous speech. The board is not usually seeking more information. The question is principally to offer you a last opportunity to present further qualifications or to indicate that you have nothing to add. So, if you feel that a significant qualification or characteristic has been overlooked, it is proper to point it out in a sentence or so. Do not compliment the board on the thoroughness of their examination – they have been sketchy, and you know it. If you wish, merely say, "No thank you, I have nothing further to add." This is a point where you can "talk yourself out" of a good impression or fail to present an important bit of information. Remember, *you close the interview yourself.*

The chairman will then say, "That is all, Mr. _____, thank you." Do not be startled; the interview is over, and quicker than you think. Thank him, gather your belongings and take your leave. Save your sigh of relief for the other side of the door.

How to put your best foot forward

Throughout this entire process, you may feel that the board individually and collectively is trying to pierce your defenses, seek out your hidden weaknesses and embarrass and confuse you. Actually, this is not true. They are obliged to make an appraisal of your qualifications for the job you are seeking, and they want to see you in your best light. Remember, they must interview all candidates and a non-cooperative candidate may become a failure in spite of their best efforts to bring out his qualifications. Here are 15 suggestions that will help you:

1) Be natural – Keep your attitude confident, not cocky

If you are not confident that you can do the job, do not expect the board to be. Do not apologize for your weaknesses, try to bring out your strong points. The board is interested in a positive, not negative, presentation. Cockiness will antagonize any board member and make him wonder if you are covering up a weakness by a false show of strength.

2) Get comfortable, but don't lounge or sprawl

Sit erectly but not stiffly. A careless posture may lead the board to conclude that you are careless in other things, or at least that you are not impressed by the importance of the occasion. Either conclusion is natural, even if incorrect. Do not fuss with your clothing, a pencil or an ashtray. Your hands may occasionally be useful to emphasize a point; do not let them become a point of distraction.

3) Do not wisecrack or make small talk

This is a serious situation, and your attitude should show that you consider it as such. Further, the time of the board is limited – they do not want to waste it, and neither should you.

4) Do not exaggerate your experience or abilities

In the first place, from information in the application or other interviews and sources, the board may know more about you than you think. Secondly, you probably will not get away with it. An experienced board is rather adept at spotting such a situation, so do not take the chance.

5) If you know a board member, do not make a point of it, yet do not hide it

Certainly you are not fooling him, and probably not the other members of the board. Do not try to take advantage of your acquaintanceship – it will probably do you little good.

6) Do not dominate the interview

Let the board do that. They will give you the clues – do not assume that you have to do all the talking. Realize that the board has a number of questions to ask you, and do not try to take up all the interview time by showing off your extensive knowledge of the answer to the first one.

7) Be attentive

You only have 20 minutes or so, and you should keep your attention at its sharpest throughout. When a member is addressing a problem or question to you, give him your undivided attention. Address your reply principally to him, but do not exclude the other board members.

8) Do not interrupt

A board member may be stating a problem for you to analyze. He will ask you a question when the time comes. Let him state the problem, and wait for the question.

9) Make sure you understand the question

Do not try to answer until you are sure what the question is. If it is not clear, restate it in your own words or ask the board member to clarify it for you. However, do not haggle about minor elements.

10) Reply promptly but not hastily

A common entry on oral board rating sheets is "candidate responded readily," or "candidate hesitated in replies." Respond as promptly and quickly as you can, but do not jump to a hasty, ill-considered answer.

11) Do not be peremptory in your answers

A brief answer is proper – but do not fire your answer back. That is a losing game from your point of view. The board member can probably ask questions much faster than you can answer them.

12) Do not try to create the answer you think the board member wants

He is interested in what kind of mind you have and how it works – not in playing games. Furthermore, he can usually spot this practice and will actually grade you down on it.

13) Do not switch sides in your reply merely to agree with a board member

Frequently, a member will take a contrary position merely to draw you out and to see if you are willing and able to defend your point of view. Do not start a debate, yet do not surrender a good position. If a position is worth taking, it is worth defending.

14) Do not be afraid to admit an error in judgment if you are shown to be wrong

The board knows that you are forced to reply without any opportunity for careful consideration. Your answer may be demonstrably wrong. If so, admit it and get on with the interview.

15) Do not dwell at length on your present job

The opening question may relate to your present assignment. Answer the question but do not go into an extended discussion. You are being examined for a *new* job, not your present one. As a matter of fact, try to phrase ALL your answers in terms of the job for which you are being examined.

Basis of Rating

Probably you will forget most of these "do's" and "don'ts" when you walk into the oral interview room. Even remembering them all will not ensure you a passing grade. Perhaps you did not have the qualifications in the first place. But remembering them will help you to put your best foot forward, without treading on the toes of the board members.

Rumor and popular opinion to the contrary notwithstanding, an oral board wants you to make the best appearance possible. They know you are under pressure – but they also want to see how you respond to it as a guide to what your reaction would be under the pressures of the job you seek. They will be influenced by the degree of poise you display, the personal traits you show and the manner in which you respond.

ABOUT THIS BOOK

This book contains tests divided into Examination Sections. Go through each test, answering every question in the margin. We have also attached a sample answer sheet at the back of the book that can be removed and used. At the end of each test look at the answer key and check your answers. On the ones you got wrong, look at the right answer choice and learn. Do not fill in the answers first. Do not memorize the questions and answers, but understand the answer and principles involved. On your test, the questions will likely be different from the samples. Questions are changed and new ones added. If you understand these past questions you should have success with any changes that arise. Tests may consist of several types of questions. We have additional books on each subject should more study be advisable or necessary for you. Finally, the more you study, the better prepared you will be. This book is intended to be the last thing you study before you walk into the examination room. Prior study of relevant texts is also recommended. NLC publishes some of these in our Fundamental Series. Knowledge and good sense are important factors in passing your exam. Good luck also helps. So now study this Passbook, absorb the material contained within and take that knowledge into the examination. Then do your best to pass that exam.

EXAMINATION SECTION

EXAMINATION SECTION
TEST 1

DIRECTIONS: Each question or incomplete statement is followed by several suggested answers or completions. Select the one that BEST answers the question or completes the statement. *PRINT THE LETTER OF THE CORRECT ANSWER IN THE SPACE AT THE RIGHT.*

1. While grinding a flat chisel, a maintainer should keep moving the chisel across the face of the grinding wheel in order to avoid 1._____

   A. burning the chisel tip
   B. mushrooming the chisel tip
   C. cracking the wheel
   D. grooving the wheel

2. Air receiver tanks are used in conjunction with a shop compressed air system PRIMARILY for the purpose of 2._____

   A. increasing the capacity of the compressor
   B. separating the stages of the compressor
   C. maintaining constant suction pressure to the compressor
   D. maintaining constant discharge pressure from the compressor

3. If a maintainer is to use a drill press in drilling a thin metal strip, he can prevent buckling of the strip if he 3._____

   A. uses the lowest drill speed available
   B. grasps the strip firmly in his hand while drilling through the strip
   C. supports the strip on blocks placed either side of the hole while drilling through the strip
   D. clamps the strip between 2 pieces of heavier stock and drills through all 3 pieces

4. The terms *bed, crosshead, front gauge,* and *back gauge* are *all* associated with 4._____

   A. bulldog shears
   B. squaring shears
   C. hand-lever punches
   D. turret punch presses

5. A maintainer should use a plug-type tap to 5._____

   A. cut threads on a pipe plug
   B. cut threads on an SAE plug
   C. thread a hole only part way
   D. thread a blind hole to its bottom

6. In order to straighten a bus frame which has been bent severely, a maintainer should apply a restoring force by utilizing a 6._____

   A. *come-along* ratchet puller-hoist
   B. *do all* rack-and-lever mechanical jack
   C. *gantry* portable hydraulic floor crane
   D. *porto-power* portable hydraulic cylinder press

7. A maintainer is drilling 1/16 inch diameter holes into a piece of 1/4 inch thick angle iron using a portable drill.
   The drill bit may break if the maintainer 7._____

   A. feeds the drill too fast
   B. tightens the chuck too much

C. drills at a speed which is too low
D. withdraws the drill from the hole too frequently

8. A riveted side panel on a certain bus has been damaged and must be replaced. The buttonhead rivets are easily accessible from the outside of the bus body.
Of the following, the BEST method for removing the rivets is to cut off the rivet heads by using a

   A. cold chisel
   B. fly cutter
   C. reamer
   D. rivet set

9. Of the following, the group of equipment which is *most often* used in repairing bus bodies is the

   A. vacuum pump, core box, drop forge, and hearth
   B. vacuum pump, drill press, dynamometer, and screw press
   C. air compressor, band saw, sander-polisher, and arc welder
   D. air compressor, radial drill, internal grinder, and milling machine

10. Of the following, the file which a maintainer should use for drawfiling and other precision work is the _____ file.

    A. mill B. round C. bastard D. triangular

11. A maintainer is to drill holes in an aluminum plate and install rivets which are 3/16 inch diameter x 1/2 inch long.
Of the following, the BEST drill size for making the rivet holes is

    A. 0.184" B. 0.191" C. 0.484" D. 0.516"

12. Assume that a maintainer is spray painting a bus body and observes that the paint finish is poor because of excessive paint dust.
To correct this condition, the maintainer should

    A. overlap his strokes
    B. move his gun closer to the surface
    C. move his gun further away from the surface
    D. reduce the amount of thinner in the paint

13. A maintainer should repair a pinhole leak in the copper tubes of a bus heater core by the process of

    A. electro-plating
    B. flaring
    C. soft-soldering
    D. oxyacetylene welding

14. A maintainer is to repair a damaged bus body by replacing a length of aluminum channel on the body support frame.
If he replaces the part with a length of steel channel of the identical dimensions, then he should know that, in comparison with the aluminum member, the steel member will deflect

    A. one-third of the amount deflected by the aluminum part
    B. the same amount deflected by the aluminum part
    C. twice the amount deflected by the aluminum part
    D. three times the amount deflected by the aluminum part

Questions 15-20

DIRECTIONS: Questions 15 to 20 are based on BULKHEAD sketched below. Consult this drawing when answering these questions.

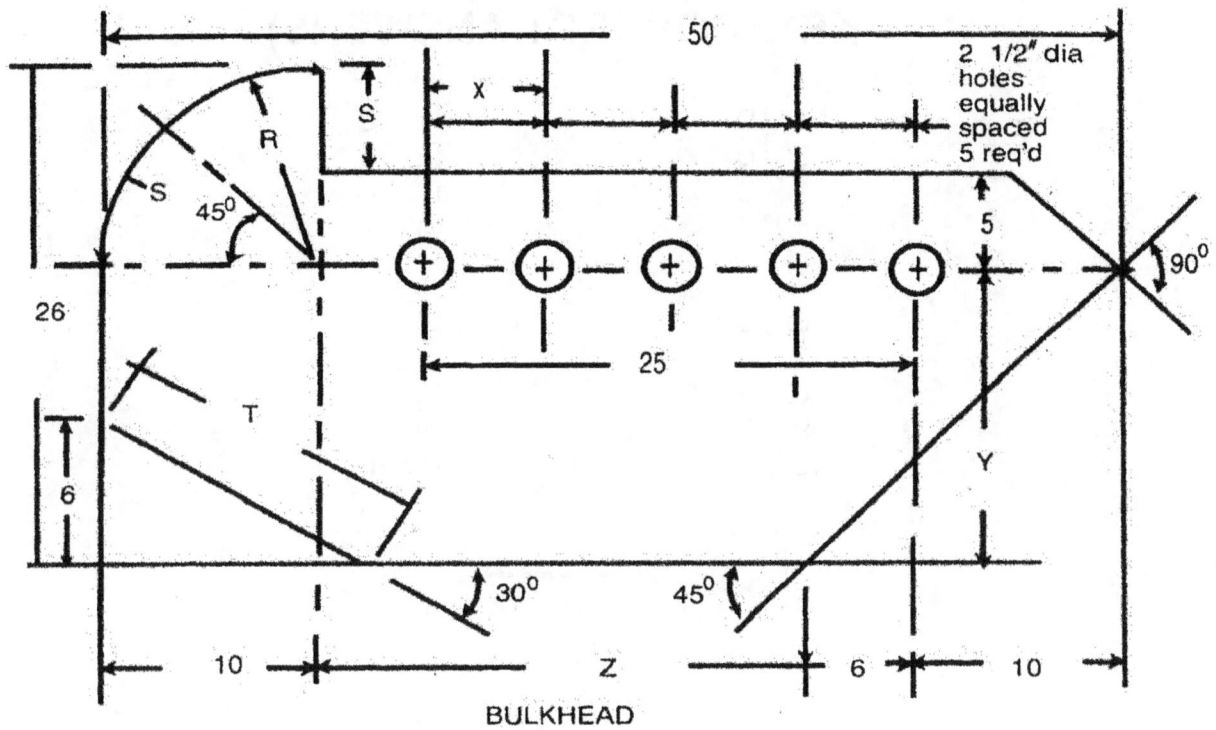

Material-Cold Rolled Steel
All dimensions in inches
(Not to scale)

15. The dimension R, in inches, is 15.____
    A. 6   B. 10   C. 16   D. 26

16. The dimension S, in inches, is, *most nearly*, 16.____
    A. 8   B. 10   C. 16   D. 20

17. The dimension T, in inches, is 17.____
    A. 8   B. 10   C. 12   D. 16

18. The dimension X, in inches, is 18.____
    A. 4 1/16   B. 4 1/4   C. 5   D. 6 1/4

19. The dimension Y, in inches, is 19.____
    A. 10   B. 12   C. 16   D. 20

20. The dimension Z, in inches, is 20.____
    A. 16   B. 24   C. 25   D. 30

KEY (CORRECT ANSWERS)

1. D
2. D
3. D
4. B
5. C

6. D
7. A
8. A
9. C
10. A

11. B
12. B
13. C
14. A
15. B

16. A
17. C
18. D
19. C
20. B

TEST 2

DIRECTIONS: Each question or incomplete statement is followed by several suggested answers or completions. Select the one that BEST answers the question or completes the statement. *PRINT THE LETTER OF THE CORRECT ANSWER IN THE SPACE AT THE RIGHT.*

1. A maintainer should repair a crack in the cast aluminum converter housing of a bus transmission by the process of

    A. metal apraying
    B. silver brazing
    C. tinning
    D. heliarc welding

2. The terms *cup, cone, flat,* and *fulldog all* refer to types of

    A. bolts
    B. common machine screws
    C. keys
    D. setscrews

3. A maintainer is to shorten a 3/4 inch diameter bolt to a given length.
   Of the following hand tools which are available to him, the maintainer should cut the bolt using the

    A. aviation snips
    B. cross-cut saw
    C. 12-inch hacksaw
    D. 18-inch bolt cutter

4. Of the following, the statement regarding the use of pliers which is *most nearly* correct is that

    A. diagonal pliers are often used to tighten hex nuts
    B. channel-lock pliers are often used in place of long-nose pliers
    C. vise-grip pliers are often used to clamp metal parts together
    D. slip-joint combination pliers are often used to cut hardened spring wire

5. A maintainer should repair leaks in the steel fuel tank of a bus by the process of

    A. electro-plating
    B. leading
    C. tinning
    D. welding

6. A maintainer is to cut off a piece from a 2-foot length of angle iron which is clamped in a vise.
   Of the following, the BEST practice while cutting the angle with a hacksaw is for the maintainer to

    A. use very short, rapid strokes
    B. keep one hand free in order to balance himself
    C. use heavy pressure on both the forward and return strokes
    D. slow the speed of cutting when the piece is almost cut through

7. Of the following, the *only* pressurized gas which could be used SAFELY as a substitute for compressed air in the maintenance shop is

    A. acetylene   B. hydrogen   C. nitrogen   D. oxygen

8. Of the following, the substance which is used to prime coat metal items before painting is

    A. brine
    B. linseed oil
    C. mineral oil
    D. zinc chromate

5

9. Of the following, the statement regarding the repainting of car bodies which is *most nearly* correct is that

   A. for the highest consistent quality of finish, repainting should start at the bare metal
   B. it is impossible to achieve a high grade of finish over an old paint finish
   C. the quality of a paint finish is determined only by the method of curing
   D. if the bare metal is rough, rubbing the final coat of paint makes the surface smooth

10. In order to operate a paint spray gun properly, a maintainer should use a(n)

    A. vacuum pump
    B. air compressor
    C. vacuum motor
    D. air motor

11. A maintainer sometimes will turn the blade of a hacksaw at right angles to the saw frame in order to

    A. remove the blade more easily
    B. increase the precision of his cut
    C. damp out vibration in the blade while cutting
    D. make a cut which is deeper than the frame of the saw

12. If a jack cannot be extended high enough to lift a certain bus, a maintainer should

    A. replace the jack handle with a longer handle
    B. place a metal extender between the jack and the bus body
    C. place a hardwood extender between the jack and the bus body
    D. place hardwood blocking between the base of the jack and the floor

13. A brass wear plate in a bus transmission has been worn by continued contact with a hardened gear until it is out of tolerance.
    In order to build up the surface of the wear plate, a maintainer should add layers of

    A. chromium plating
    B. soft solder
    C. copper solder
    D. welded steel

14. Annealing is a process that consists of

    A. reheating a hardened piece of metal to a certain point, then plunging it into cold water
    B. heating a soft metal object to a red heat and then cooling it quickly by plunging it into brine
    C. raising a piece of metal to a high temperature and then hammering it into any desired shape
    D. heating a metal piece to a high and uniform temperature and then allowing it to cool slowly in air

15. Sheet metal of 0.051 inch thickness is to be riveted to a 1" x 1" x 1/8" angle, using 1/8 inch diameter rivets. In order to form the proper head, the rivets used for this job should have a shank length of, *most nearly,*

    A. 1/8"   B. 3/16"   C. 3/8"   D. 1 1/8"

16. The number of complete circular pieces, 9 1/2 inches in diameter, which can be cut from a metal sheet, 5 feet by 10 feet, is, *most nearly,*

    A. 50   B. 70   C. 95   D. 100

17. Of the following, the statement concerning the installation of rivets which is CORRECT is   17.____
    that

    A. the head is formed on a blind rivet by hammering with a rivet set
    B. the head is formed on a tinner's rivet by hammering with a rivet set
    C. a blind rivet is upset by hammering with a rivet set
    D. a tinner's rivet must be used where there is no access to the reverse side of the work

18. A maintainer should attach the ends of new copper tubes into a steel header of a bus   18.____
    heat exchanger by the process of

    A. electro-plating   B. silver brazing
    C. oxyacetylene welding   D. hard-soldering

19. Assume that a maintainer observes runs and snags in the finish of a panel which he is   19.____
    spray painting.
    Of the following, the *most likely* cause for runs and snags in the finish is that he

    A. did not overlap his strokes
    B. held his gun too far from the surface of the panel
    C. held his gun too close to the surface of the panel
    D. kept his gun moving over the entire surface of the panel

20. A maintainer is to join two mild sheets with rivets. For the STRONGEST joint, he should   20.____
    use rivets made of

    A. aluminum   B. brass   C. copper   D. steel

KEY (CORRECT ANSWERS)

1. D   11. D
2. D   12. D
3. C   13. A
4. C   14. D
5. D   15. C

6. D   16. B
7. C   17. B
8. D   18. B
9. A   19. C
10. B   20. D

EXAMINATION SECTION
TEST 1

DIRECTIONS: Each question or incomplete statement is followed by several suggested answers or completions. Select the one that BEST answers the question or completes the statement. *PRINT THE LETTER OF THE CORRECT ANSWER IN THE SPACE AT THE RIGHT.*

1. The addition of turpentine to paint in order to make painting easier is known as

   A. bleeding   B. cutting   C. setting   D. thinning

2. Assume that a maintainer observes pin holes in the finish of a bus which he is spray painting. Of the following, the *most likely* cause for pin holes in the finish is

   A. insufficient thinner
   B. oil in the air lines
   C. insufficient drying time
   D. excessive pigment in the finish

3. When using a slip roll forming machine, a maintainer should adjust for the thickness of the metal stock being formed by adjusting the _____ adjusting screws.

   A. lower roll   B. upper roll
   C. rear roll   D. upper release

4. A maintainer is to make a frame for a sign using 2" x 2" x 1/8" angle iron. The *most practical* method of forming a 90-degree corner is to

   A. bend the angle cold, on a power press, before cutting
   B. make a vee-cut in one log of the angle before bending
   C. cut a triangular corner on each leg and weld the legs together to form the frame
   D. heat until the angle is cherry red and bend before cutting

5. The terms *common-square, dividers, prick punch,* and *scratch awl* are ALL associated with _____ tools.

   A. glazing   B. metal layout
   C. metal cutting   D. wood turning

6. The terms *cape, diamond-point, half-round* and *round-nose* ALL refer to

   A. chisels   B. files   C. hammers   D. pliers

7. Assume that a maintainer plans to shrink a certain section of a steel sheet which has been stretched out of shape.
   If the maintainer heats the sheet until it is cherry red, the result will be that the steel sheet will

   A. stretch further upon cooling in the air
   B. become hardened upon cooling in the air
   C. melt to form a hole in the center of the heated area
   D. lose its temper or springiness

8. When two pieces of sheet metal are being soldered together, it is important that they be clamped to prevent movement.
It is *also* IMPORTANT to

   A. keep the joint cool with a large heat sink
   B. put insulation between the metal clamp and the sheets
   C. reheat the solder after it has cooled
   D. test the joint strength while the joint is cooling

9. Assume that while using arc welding equipment to repair a crack in a cast steel housing, a maintainer carelessly drops the electrode holder on to his metal work table. The carelessness by the maintainer will, *most likely*, result in a

   A. shorted circuit in the welding machine
   B. loss of pressure from the gas cylinder
   C. broken grounding clamp
   D. melted gas supply hose

10. Assume that a maintainer is applying molten solder to a joint between two pieces of copper.
For a SOUND joint, he should

    A. pour cold water over the hot joint
    B. pour cold oil over the hot joint
    C. allow the solder to cool slowly in air
    D. reheat the joint several times before cooling

11. How many 9 1/2 inch long pieces of copper tubing can be cut from a 20-foot length of tubing?

    A. 24   B. 25   C. 26   D. 27

12. Two splice plates must be cut from a piece of sheet steel that has an overall length of 14 3/8 inches. The plates are to be 7 5/8 inches and 5 1/4 inches long.
If 1/16 inch is allowed for each saw cut, then how much material would be left?

    A. 1 3/8"   B. 1 1/2"   C. 1 5/8"   D. 1 3/4"

13. A maintainer requires several lengths of tubing for oil lines as follows: 12 7/16 inches, 14 5/16 inches, 9 3/16 inches, 9 1/8 inches, 6 1/4 inches, and 5 inches.
The TOTAL LENGTH of tubing required is, *most nearly*, _____ feet.

    A. 2   B. 3   C. 4   D. 5

14. After a maintainer sets up the oxygen and acetylene gas cylinders for welding, he should check for leaks by

    A. holding a lighted match near the hose connections
    B. using a halide torch
    C. coating all connections with soap suds
    D. coating all connections with grease

15. Plastic filler material can be used to restore the surface of damaged metal body panels. One of the properties of this material is that plastic fillers

    A. harden at room temperature and can be sanded smooth
    B. make joints which are as strong as the base metal in the panel
    C. melt and flow into a smooth finish when heated with a torch
    D. must be applied with a special soldering iron

15.____

16. If a maintainer is to use the oxyacetylene torch to cut steel, he should obtain the HOTTEST flame by supplying

    A. an excess of acetylene
    B. an excess of oxygen
    C. an excess of carbon
    D. equal amounts of acetylene and oxygen

16.____

17. Of the following, it would be most difficult to soft solder a copper wire to a metal sheet of

    A. aluminum   B. brass   C. mild steel   D. tin

17.____

18. One of the MAIN reasons for using welding rods with a flux coating is to

    A. float impurities out of the puddle
    B. accelerate the cooling of the weld metal
    C. form a blanket of oxygen over the arc and the molten metal
    D. form a blanket of moist air over the arc and the molten metal

18.____

19. Flux should be left on a weld deposit during cooling in order to

    A. prevent the formation of slag
    B. trap the gases so they will not escape
    C. slow the cooling of the weld metal
    D. accelerate the cooling of the weld metal

19.____

20. If a nut is turned six complete turns on a 3/8 - 24 NF bolt, it will advance a distance of

    A. 1/4"   B. 3/8"   C. 24/32"   D. 1 1/2"

20.____

KEY (CORRECT ANSWERS)

1.	D	11.	B
2.	B	12.	A
3.	A	13.	D
4.	B	14.	C
5.	B	15.	A
6.	A	16.	B
7.	D	17.	A
8.	B	18.	A
9.	A	19.	C
10.	C	20.	A

TEST 2

DIRECTIONS: Each question or incomplete statement is followed by several suggested answers or completions. Select the one that BEST answers the question or completes the statement. *PRINT THE LETTER OF THE CORRECT ANSWER IN THE SPACE AT THE RIGHT.*

1. The door of an automobile locks when the lock engages the

    A. door check
    B. door panel flange
    C. hinge plate
    D. striker plate

    1._____

2. If the total time allowance for replacing the glass in a broken bus window is 75 minutes, how many jobs of this kind would a maintainer be expected to do in 40 hours of work?

    A. 32   B. 40   C. 60   D. 72

    2._____

3. A certain rod is tapered so that it changes diameter at a rate of 1/4 inch per foot of length. If the tapered rod is 3 inches long, then the DIFFERENCE in diameter between the two ends is, *most nearly,*

    A. 0.250"   B. 0.187"   C. 0.135"   D. 0.062"

    3._____

4. If a maintainer is setting up a gas welding torch, he should be careful to connect the _____ hose to the _____ cylinder.

    A. green; acetylene
    B. green; oxygen
    C. black; acetylene
    D. black; hydrogen

    4._____

5. Assume that a maintainer is to rivet two metal sheets together to form a lap joint which will have a maximum resistance to tearing.
The joint is LEAST LIKELY to tear if the distance measured from the center of the rivet hole to the edge of each sheet is, *at least,*

    A. equal to the diameter of the rivet hole
    B. twice the diameter of the rivet hole
    C. equal to the thickness of the plate material
    D. four times the thickness of the plate material

    5._____

6. Six equally spaced holes are to be drilled in a flat steel sheet on a common center line between two fixed points.
The PROPER tool to use in laying out the centers of the holes is a

    A. hole punch
    B. hollow punch
    C. pair of calipers
    D. pair of dividers

    6._____

7. In order to produce a carburizing flame with an oxyacetylene torch, a maintainer should

    A. supply an excess of oxygen gas
    B. supply an excess of acetylene gas
    C. supply equal parts of oxygen and acetylene gases
    D. decrease the amount of both the oxygen and acetylene gases

    7._____

8. A maintainer is to make a silver brazed tube and flange assembly as shown in the sketch.
The GREATEST joint strength will result from a joint clearance C of, *most nearly,*

    8._____

A. 0.001" to 0.005"
B. 0.010" to 0.020"
C. 0.025" to 0.050"
D. 0.050" to 0.075"

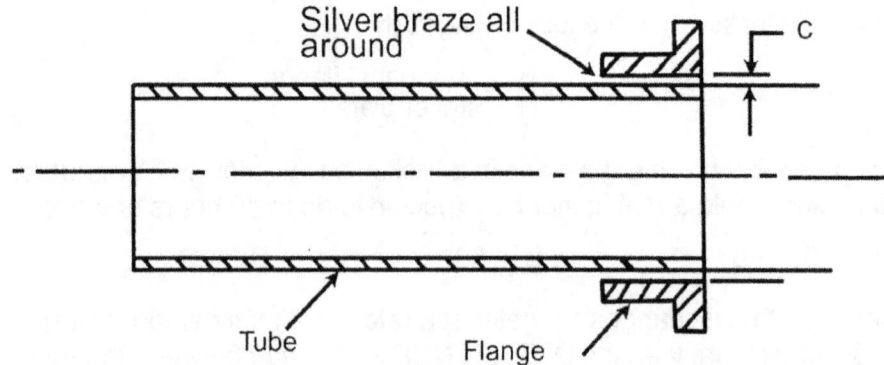

9. Assume that a maintainer is sent on an emergency road call to perform arc welding repairs at a location where there is no electrical power available.
The type of welder that must be used where there is no electrical power available is the _____ type.

   A. transformer
   B. rectifier
   C. transformer-rectifier
   D. engine driven generator

9.____

10. Of the following, the type of fire extinguisher which should be used on electrical fires is the _____ type.

   A. dry chemical   B. foam
   C. pumped water   D. soda-acid

10.____

11. After silver brazing a copper based alloy gear, a maintainer should remove the flux by flushing the joint with

   A. activated rosin   B. carbon tetrachloride
   C. hot water   D. muriatic acid

11.____

12. The type of hammer which a maintainer would use to remove small dents in sheet metal panels is the _____ hammer.

   A. ball peen   B. claw   C. dinging   D. maul

12.____

13. If a maintainer observes that a cylinder which is used for storing compressed gas has been marked in chalk with the letters *MT*, then he should know that this gas cylinder

   A. no longer contains a pressurized gas
   B. is a special type used only by the transit authority
   C. must be stored on a moving truck by resting on one side
   D. must be connected to a torch which has left-hand threads

13.____

Questions 14-15.

DIRECTIONS: Questions 14 and 15 are based on the two views of a rectangular pipe shown below. Consult these views when answering these questions.

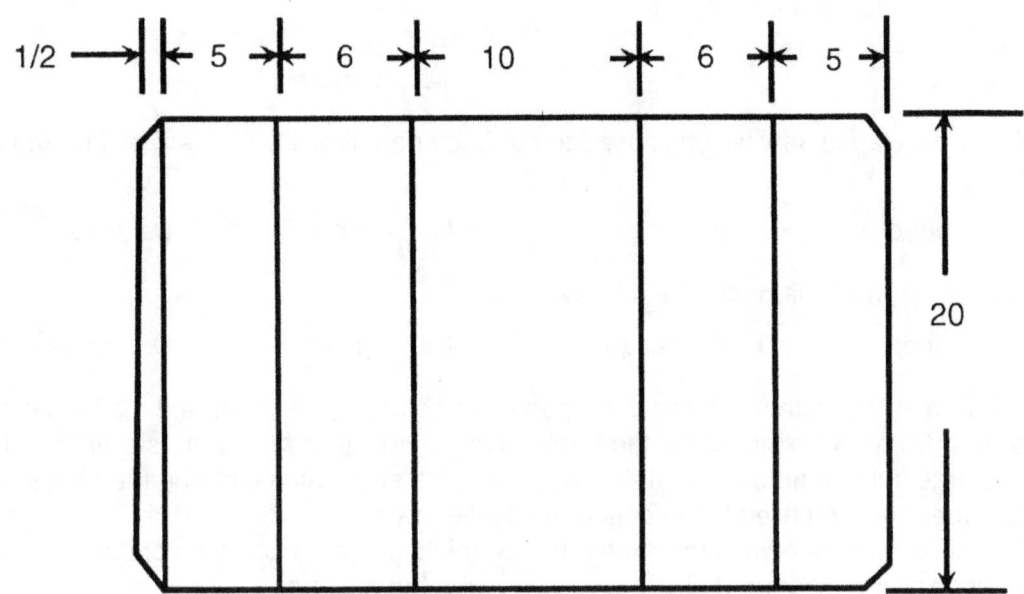

STRETCHOUT OF RECTANGULAR PIPE

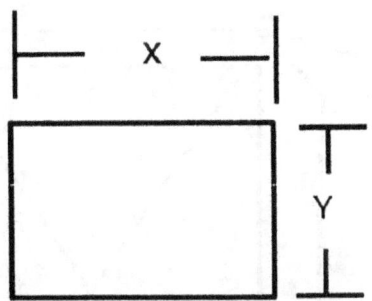

END VIEW OF RECTANGULAR PIPE

14. The dimension X in the sketch is *equivalent* to the number 14._____
    A. 1/2   B. 5   C. 6   D. 10

15. The dimension Y in the sketch is *equivalent* to the number 15._____
    A. 1/2   B. 6   C. 10   D. 20

16. Certain metals used in body repair work are known as *ferrous metals* because they contain 16._____
    A. brass   B. chromium   C. iron   D. nickel

17. A maintainer must hold the pieces of a metal frame in a certain specified alignment while welding them together. A mechanical device which will hold the pieces in the *exact* alignment is a   17.___

    A. dolly block   B. die
    C. jig   D. mandrel

18. A narrow bladed saw which is used to cut body panels while they are still on the bus is the _____ saw.   18.___

    A. band   B. saber   C. nibbler   D. cutoff

19. A liquid in which paint can be dissolved is a   19.___

    A. drier   B. lacquer   C. pigment   D. solvent

20. After an automobile has been damaged in an accident, an observant maintainer can recognize from visible signs that the frame is bent. However, his diagnosis will be more accurate if the maintainer makes measurements at certain points on the chassis which can then be compared for evidence of misalignment.   20.___
On the chassis shown in the sketch below, misalignment should be checked by comparison of the measured distance _____ with the distance _____.

    A. PX; XS   B. RY; XS   C. PX; SZ   D. RY; SZ

CHECKING CHASSIS ALIGNMENT

KEY (CORRECT ANSWERS)

1. D
2. A
3. D
4. B
5. B

6. D
7. B
8. A
9. D
10. A

11. C
12. C
13. A
14. D
15. B

16. C
17. C
18. B
19. D
20. B

EXAMINATION SECTION
TEST 1

DIRECTIONS: Each question or incomplete statement is followed by several suggested answers or completions. Select the one that BEST answers the question or completes the statement. *PRINT THE LETTER OF THE CORRECT ANSWER IN THE SPACE AT THE RIGHT.*

1. Holes drilled for use with pull rods should be _____ in diameter. 1.____
   A. 15/32"   B. 1/4"   C. 9/64"   D. 7/48"

2. Which type of paint compound is MOST often used as a general purpose finisher for spot repair on all types of automobile finishes? 2.____
   A. Acrylic lacquer B. Acrylic enamel
   C. Synthetic enamel D. Urethane enamel

3. What is the MAXIMUM temperature (°F) that can be applied to a frame member to aid in straightening? 3.____
   A. 800   B. 1200   C. 1750   D. 2000

4. If a panel has not been *banded in,* at what point during the refinishing stroke should the sprayer trigger be pulled? 4.____
   A. Just before the edge of the panel
   B. Right at the edge of the panel
   C. Just after the sprayer has passed the edge
   D. At the center, working outward toward one edge at a time

5. Each of the following is a typical effect of a bent or shifted upper door hinge EXCEPT 5.____
   A. drop-off at belt line on lock pillar
   B. overlap on adjoining panel
   C. v-shaped edge gap that is wider at the bottom end
   D. widened edge gap at front of bottom horizontal gap

6. Which type of weld joins two pieces of metal together at the line where they are placed alongside each other? 6.____
   A. Butt   B. Tack   C. Fillet   D. Plug

7. When spreading repair jelly to fix rust spots, the work should begin at the 7.____
   A. center, gradually moving outward
   B. outer edge, moving inward
   C. top, working downward
   D. side opposite the hand holding the spreader, working horizontally

8. What is the typical range of atomizing pressure (lbs.) used for automotive spray refinishing? 8.____
   A. 15-25   B. 30-60   C. 75-90   D. 95-120

9. What grit of abrasive is USUALLY recommended for sanding a primer coat?

   A. 80   B. 100   C. 160   D. 280

10. When welding with an acetylene torch, the inner cone of the flame should be held _____ from the working surface.

    A. 1/2"   B. 1"   C. 2"   D. 3"

11. Which type of spray gun is BEST for the application of large amounts of a single color of finish material?

    A. Internal mix
    B. External mix
    C. Suction feed
    D. Pressure feed

12. When using solder to fill in dents on auto bodies, the melting point of the solder should be _____ °F.

    A. 361-437   B. 469-543   C. 500-569   D. 569-670

13. What is the MAIN advantage associated with using a belt sander for preparing a metal surface?

    A. Dust collection
    B. Maneuverability
    C. Adaptable to slightly curved surfaces
    D. Increased sensitivity to low or high spots

14. What fluid tip size, in inches, is MOST commonly used with suction feed spray guns?

    A. .100   B. .072   C. .041   D. .028

15. Which of the abrasives below is MOST commonly used for auto body reconditioning and refinishing?

    A. Emery
    B. Flint quartz
    C. Silicon carbide
    D. Crocus

16. The normal thickness of the undercoat for an automotive finish is _____ inch.

    A. .100   B. .012   C. .004   D. .002

17. What practice is used to remove uneven or jagged edges from a metal piece?

    A. Buffing   B. Beading   C. Filing   D. Deburring

18. Windshield caulking material normally begins to cure or dry _____ minutes after it has been applied.

    A. 15   B. 30   C. 45   D. 60

19. Which device should be used to repair or straighten a sheet metal surface in constricted areas where it is not possible to use a conventional dolly?

    A. Beading tool
    B. Spoon
    C. File holder
    D. Solder paddle

20. Which of the following steps in welding two panels together would occur FIRST? 20.____

    A. Metal finish applied to surfaces on either side of the weld
    B. Tinning applied over weld
    C. Weld hammered below metal surface
    D. Solder over weld

21. The MAIN disadvantage of using abrasive wheels to cut metal is 21.____

    A. relative slowness
    B. fire hazard
    C. difficulty in handling curves of small radius
    D. increased amount of wasted metal

22. What is a tack rag used for? 22.____

    A. Cleaning a spray gun
    B. Holding upholstery tacks
    C. Applying rubbing compounds
    D. Wiping dust from surface before spraying

23. What grit of abrasive is MOST commonly used with orbital sanders? 23.____

    A. 40   B. 60   C. 80   D. 120

24. When covering a rusted area with fiber glass, the purpose of drilling holes through the metal is to 24.____

    A. prepare for use with pull rods
    B. provide better adhesion
    C. provide attachment points for fiber glass
    D. allow for expansion

25. The usual clearance between the door and surrounding frame of an auto body is between _____ inch. 25.____

    A. 1/8-5/32   B. 7/32-1/4   C. 1/4-3/16   D. 3/8-1/2

KEY (CORRECT ANSWERS)

1. C
2. A
3. B
4. B
5. C

6. A
7. A
8. B
9. D
10. B

11. D
12. A
13. A
14. C
15. C

16. D
17. D
18. A
19. B
20. C

21. C
22. D
23. C
24. B
25. A

TEST 2

DIRECTIONS: Each question or incomplete statement is followed by several suggested answers or completions. Select the one that BEST answers the question or completes the statement. *PRINT THE LETTER OF THE CORRECT ANSWER IN THE SPACE AT THE RIGHT.*

1. When repaneling a car door, which of the following steps would occur LAST? 1._____

   A. Seal hem-flange
   B. Assemble inner and outer panel with sealer beading
   C. Straighten facings and safety beams
   D. Turn hem-flange

2. What is the term for a cutout metal piece prepared for fabrication? 2._____

   A. Blank   B. Buck   C. Panel   D. Block

3. Which of the following steps in the welding of a damaged rocker panel would occur FIRST? 3._____

   A. Complete seam with 1/2 inch welds
   B. Tack weld outer edges and check alignment
   C. Weld upper and lower flange to inner panel
   D. Add tack welds in skip pattern

4. What is the PREFERRED shape of the tip of a soldering iron used to fill pull-rod holes? 4._____

   A. Conventional pyramid   B. Blunt
   C. Flat blade   D. Long rounded taper

5. When using a dry disk sander to produce an enamel finish on a repainting job, what grit of abrasive is recommended? 5._____

   A. 180   B. 240   C. 320   D. 400

6. Each of the following is needed for the repair of a crumpled rear quarter panel EXCEPT a 6._____

   A. pick hammer   B. spreader
   C. body file   D. glazing putty

7. *Flop* is described as 7._____

   A. the difference in finish color when viewed straight on and at angles
   B. the warp effect caused by overjacking a damaged frame
   C. the overlapping of door and panel edges caused by a damaged hinge
   D. gaps in seals caused by misalignment of door window glass

8. What is the MINIMUM number of frame gauges or sight lines that should be used to locate the misalignment of a frame? 8._____

   A. 2   B. 3   C. 4   D. 5

9. The rear height of a car hood is NORMALLY adjusted by means of

   A. hood pin
   B. hinge bolts
   C. base of hood lock
   D. stop screws

10. In order to prepare a piece of sheet metal for fastening, the edges of a drilled hole are sometimes turned downward in order to better accept the fastener.
    This is known as

    A. spooning   B. dimpling   C. crowning   D. bucking

11. At what temperature (° F) is brazing done with a non-ferrous filler rod?

    A. 400   B. 800   C. 1800   D. 2800

12. How should the graining effect be restored to a damaged vinyl top?

    A. Etching with the tip of a soldering iron
    B. Stamping with a die sent by the manufacturer
    C. Injected with a hypodermic needle
    D. Splicing in a new piece of material

13. When using power tools, what gauge of wire should be used for a 50-foot extension cable if the current is 5 amperes?

    A. 8   B. 10   C. 12   D. 18

14. Which type of spray gun is BEST for the application of fast-drying finish materials?

    A. Internal mix
    B. External mix
    C. Suction feed
    D. Pressure feed

15. What is the common or recommended distance between holes that are drilled for use with pull rods?

    A. 9/32"   B. 1/4"   C. 9/64"   D. 1/8"

16. A *bumping* spoon is used as a dolly PRIMARILY for

    A. small, high-crown dents
    B. long, relatively smooth buckles
    C. peaked ridges at the edges of large impact dents
    D. short creases in tight, hard-to-reach spots

17. For automotive refinishing, large spray gun systems should use a fluid hose with an inside diameter of _____ inch.

    A. 1/4   B. 1/2   C. 5/16   D. 7/8

18. When repairing a scratch or gouge in fiber glass paneling, the applied filler should be shrunk by means of

    A. application of liquid nitrogen
    B. coating with epoxy resin
    C. allowing to stand for 24 hours
    D. using a heat gun

19. Which system for straightening automobile frames uses a flat reference plane consisting of specially designed steel members set into the shop floor?   19._____

    A. Stationary rack B. Korek
    C. Dozer D. Rail

20. Water drain holes are located in each of the following body components EXCEPT   20._____

    A. doors B. rocker panels
    C. quarter panels D. deck lids

21. What is the MAIN difference between a shrinking hammer and an ordinary dinging hammer?   21._____

    A. Weight of head B. Length of handle
    C. Cross-grooved head D. Length of head

22. When refinishing a car hood, spraying should begin at the   22._____

    A. side nearest the sprayer
    B. side farthest from the sprayer
    C. center
    D. side opposite the hand holding the sprayer

23. Which type of weld is considered a temporary fastening that is meant to hold pieces in place for final welding?   23._____

    A. Butt B. Tack C. Fillet D. Plug

24. The normal thickness of a complete automotive finish is _____ inch.   24._____

    A. .100 B. .012 C. .004 D. .002

25. Each of the following is needed for the repair of minor surface scratches EXCEPT   25._____

    A. 320-grit dry abrasive B. 400-grit wet abrasive
    C. primer D. body filler

4 (#2)

KEY (CORRECT ANSWERS)

1. A
2. A
3. C
4. D
5. B

6. A
7. A
8. B
9. B
10. B

11. B
12. A
13. D
14. B
15. B

16. B
17. B
18. D
19. B
20. D

21. C
22. A
23. B
24. C
25. D

EXAMINATION SECTION
TEST 1

DIRECTIONS: Each question or incomplete statement is followed by several suggested answers or completions. Select the one that BEST answers the question or completes the statement. *PRINT THE LETTER OF THE CORRECT ANSWER IN THE SPACE AT THE RIGHT.*

1. What is the metalworking term for a reference mark used to accurately fit or join two separate parts? 1.____

    A. Tangent
    B. Bend line
    C. Witness line
    D. Orbital

2. Spot welding is a method for joining two overlapping pieces of sheet metal. When joining two pieces with a series of resistance spot welds, how far apart should the welds be?
    _____ inch(es). 2.____

    A. $\frac{1}{2}$ B. 1 C. 3 D. 5

3. What type of sander is used PRIMARILY for finish sanding of metal and painted surfaces? 3.____

    A. Portable disk
    B. Rotary flexible shaft
    C. Orbital
    D. Belt

4. When using an acetylene torch, what color flame indicates an excess of acetylene in the mixture? 4.____

    A. Red B. Yellow C. Blue D. Green

5. The overall height of a raised, curved area is known as its 5.____

    A. buck B. bed depth C. crown D. slope

6. When realigning the underbody of an automobile, the under-body must be straightened to within _____ of an inch of the manufacturer's specified dimensions. 6.____

    A. 1/32 B. 1/16 C. 1/8 D. 3/8

7. Which type of paint compound is used PRIMARILY in the refinishing of commercial vehicles? 7.____

    A. Acrylic lacquer
    B. Acrylic enamel
    C. Synthetic enamel
    D. Urethane enamel

8. File holders adjust to different arcs by means of a 8.____

    A. setscrew
    B. sliding hammer
    C. spring lock
    D. turnbuckle

9. A _____ is used to take up slack in chains that are used with frame racks. 9.____

    A. twin pull hook
    B. chain lock head
    C. double-grab hook
    D. lynch pin

10. When welding a replacement panel in place, welding should start at the _____ of the panel.

    A. top B. center
    C. right edge D. left edge

11. Before spray refinishing an automobile, masking paper is applied with tape.
    What temperature (°F) is considered a MINIMUM for the application of masking tape to an auto body?

    A. 15 B. 32 C. 50 D. 72

12. Which type of weld joins two pieces of overlaying metal through a hole in the upper piece?

    A. Butt B. Tack C. Fillet D. Plug

13. The distance an upper die travels down into a lower die is referred to as

    A. stroke B. penetration
    C. throat depth D. bed width

14. Which type of abrasive is used almost exclusively as a polishing agent?

    A. Garnet B. Aluminum oxide
    C. Crocus D. Silicon carbide

15. The usual clearance between the hood and fender of an auto body is _____ inch.

    A. 1/8 B. 3/16 C. 5/32 D. 1/4

16. What procedure is used to tell whether a car is finished with nitrocellulose lacquer or acrylic?

    A. Rub surface with thinner
    B. Rub surface with manufacturer's rubbing compound
    C. Coat test spot surfaces with a layer of each compound
    D. Rub surface with silicone polish remover

17. The overall head length of a dinging hammer is USUALLY _____ inches.

    A. 2-3 B. 4-6 C. 6-8 D. 8-10

18. What is the MOST commonly used method for paint removal associated with auto body refinishing?

    A. Sandblasting B. Hot caustic solution
    C. Disk grinder D. Paint remover

19. Which of the following steps in welding two panels together would occur LAST?

    A. Metal finish applied to surfaces on either side of the weld
    B. Tinning applied over weld
    C. Weld hammered below metal surface
    D. Solder over weld

20. When using a torch to shrink metal, heat spots should be at a MAXIMUM distance of _____ apart.

    A. 1"   B. 5/8"   C. 3/8"   D. 1/4"

21. *Feather-edging* can be BEST described as

    A. filing of sheet metal edges in preparation for a fillet weld
    B. detailing practice of applying trim molding along panel sides
    C. sanding around edges of existing paint surface to prepare for refinishing
    D. repairing rust spots at panel, hood, and trunk seams

22. A repairman working to restore or straighten damaged sheet metal with a dinging hammer USUALLY strikes about _____ blows each minute.

    A. 25   B. 50   C. 100   D. 150

23. What is the cause of *creep* in a straightened automobile frame?

    A. Overjacking
    B. Lack of or insufficient heating during straightening
    C. Incorrect anchor spots
    D. Too much slack during tie-down

24. When attaching a pulling chain to an auto frame, what should be used to pad corners where the chain wraps around the frame section?

    A. Molded rubber pads
    B. Shop towels
    C. Used head gaskets
    D. Short pieces of angle iron

25. Once a new windshield has been installed and aligned, the seal should be water tested

    A. immediately
    B. 15 minutes after installation
    C. 30 minutes after installation
    D. 1 hour after installation

KEY (CORRECT ANSWERS)

1.	C	11.	C
2.	B	12.	D
3.	C	13.	A
4.	B	14.	C
5.	C	15.	C
6.	B	16.	D
7.	C	17.	B
8.	D	18.	C
9.	C	19.	D
10.	B	20.	B

21. C
22. C
23. B
24. D
25. A

TEST 2

DIRECTIONS: Each question or incomplete statement is followed by several suggested answers or completions. Select the one that BEST answers the question or completes the statement. *PRINT THE LETTER OF THE CORRECT ANSWER IN THE SPACE AT THE RIGHT.*

1. What is the term for a hardened metal bar held against a rivet stem while setting rivets to facilitate formation of a *shop head*? 1.____

   A. Dolly   B. Blank   C. Spoon   D. Buck

2. When refinishing a body surface, bleeder sealer is used to 2.____

   A. seal off scratches
   B. provide adhesion on rusted surfaces
   C. moisture-seal panel seams
   D. prevent red shades from bleeding through following coats

3. Which tool should be used to raise low spots or small dents that are revealed after surface filing? 3.____

   A. Pick hammer   B. Pick tool
   C. Fender beading tool   D. Spoon

4. What grit of abrasive is recommended for grinding solder? 4.____

   A. 16   B. 24   C. 40   D. 60

5. If specialized tramming equipment is not available for the realignment of a frame, points on the frame should be transferred to the floor by means of a 5.____

   A. straight level   B. tape measure
   C. plumb bob   D. T-square

6. What type of flame is used to weld sheet metal? 6.____

   A. Carburizing   B. Oxidizing
   C. Reducing   D. Neutral

7. When straightening/repairing a damaged piece of sheet metal, a repairman should begin straightening at the 7.____

   A. point of impact
   B. shallowest ridge nearest the point of impact
   C. deepest ridge farthest from the point of impact
   D. deepest ridge, regardless of its location

8. Door arm rests are NORMALLY attached by means of 8.____

   A. screws on the underside of the arm rest
   B. special spring clips
   C. cap screws through the inner door panel
   D. tapered pins

9. Which type of spray gun is used PRIMARILY for finish jobs involving many color changes?

    A. Internal mix
    B. External mix
    C. Suction feed
    D. Pressure feed

10. Which type of weld joins two pieces of metal at an angle to each other?

    A. Butt   B. Tack   C. Fillet   D. Plug

11. When using a stationary rack, _____ are normally used for straightening an automobile frame.

    A. steam hammers
    B. spring-lock levers
    C. screw jacks
    D. hydraulic jacks

12. Each of the following is a potential cause of *backfiring* in an acetylene torch EXCEPT

    A. lighting with a match
    B. overheated tip or nozzle
    C. operation at incorrect pressure
    D. touching tip or nozzle to working surface

13. Which tool is used to locate high and low spots on a sheet metal surface?

    A. Dolly
    B. Fender file
    C. Spoon
    D. Sander

14. A hypodermic needle is used in the repair of a damaged vinyl top to

    A. extract moisture
    B. inject adhesive
    C. inject liquid vinyl into the material
    D. bleed air from bubbles

15. If dents, pits or hammer marks cannot be removed from a metal surface before repainting, the marks should be sanded with

    A. the toe of a small belt sander
    B. the corner of an orbital sander
    C. an octagonal-shaped disk
    D. a wet, heavy-grit disk

16. What type of lubricant should be used on the fluid needle packing, air valve packing, and bearing screw of a paint spray gun?

    A. Light oil
    B. Transmission lubricant
    C. Petrolatum
    D. Wheel bearing grease

17. What is the term used by metalworkers to describe the beginning or end of a curved bend?

    A. Crown   B. Tangent   C. Flange   D. Temper

18. What is the MOST common cause of a door window's inability to raise or lower (sticking)?

   A. Lack of lubrication
   B. Wrong type of weatherstripping
   C. Wrong type of windlass
   D. Misalignment

19. When repaneling a car door, which of the following steps would occur FIRST?

   A. Seal hem-flange
   B. Assemble inner and outer panel with sealer beading
   C. Straighten facings and safety beams
   D. Turn hem-flange

20. When metal is bent beyond its elastic limit, it is considered to be

   A. tempered   B. bucked
   C. point set   D. work-hardened

21. When cutting sheet metal with an oxygen-acetylene torch, the pale blue core for preheating flame should be kept about _____ away from the metal surface.

   A. 1/16"   B. 1/8"   C. 1/4"   D. 3/8"

22. What type of flame is used for shrinking metal with an acetylene-oxygen torch?

   A. Carburizing   B. Oxidizing
   C. Reducing   D. Neutral

23. When using a rotary sander, a repairman should use the machine with

   A. brief, swift swiping motions
   B. gentle circular motions
   C. long, sweeping motions
   D. sustained pressure, one spot at a time

24. When spraying synthetic enamels, what is the CORRECT distance, in inches, between the gun and the work?

   A. 4-6   B. 6-8   C. 8-10   D. 10-12

25. A front fender is USUALLY attached to the rest of the vehicle by means of

   A. bolts   B. sheet metal screws
   C. rivets   D. spot welds

KEY (CORRECT ANSWERS)

1. D
2. D
3. A
4. B
5. C

6. D
7. C
8. A
9. C
10. C

11. D
12. A
13. B
14. D
15. C

16. A
17. B
18. D
19. C
20. D

21. A
22. B
23. C
24. C
25. A

EXAMINATION SECTION
TEST 1

DIRECTIONS: Each question or incomplete statement is followed by several suggested answers or completions. Select the one that BEST answers the question or completes the statement. *PRINT THE LETTER OF THE CORRECT ANSWER IN THE SPACE AT THE RIGHT.*

1. To check whether the working surface of a machine is horizontal, it is BEST to use a 1.____

   A. straight edge
   B. surface gage
   C. spirit level
   D. plumb bob

2. The BASIC function of an idler gear in a gear train is to change 2.____

   A. from rotary motion to linear motion
   B. direction of rotation
   C. speed of rotation
   D. from linear motion to rotary motion

3. A ½-inch portable electric drill machine, rated for one horsepower, will NOT 3.____

   A. be powerful enough to drill into a concrete wall
   B. be powerful enough to drill into a steel plate
   C. drill a hole larger than ½" diameter
   D. hold a drill with a shank larger than ½" diameter

4. Of the following screws, the one that has the LARGEST outside diameter is 4.____

   A. 10 - 32 x 3"
   B. 12 - 24 x 1¼"
   C. 12 - 28 x 1½"
   D. 1/4 - 20 x 2"

5. The ADVANTAGE of using a wrench with a ratchet handle for tightening a nut is that 5.____

   A. a greater amount of force can be applied
   B. there is less probability of rounding the corners of the nut
   C. there is less probability of the wrench slipping off the nut
   D. the socket does not have to be raised off the nut to get another *bite*

6. The PROPER instrument to use for measuring the thickness of a piece of shim stock is a 6.____

   A. feeler gage
   B. height gage
   C. standard micrometer
   D. protractor

7. A drill gage is used for measuring a drill 7.____

   A. angle of twist
   B. cutting angle
   C. speed
   D. diameter

8. The liquid in the heavy duty lifting jacks used in shops is

   A. alcohol B. mercury C. oil D. water

9. A gear box has been reassembled and the gears do not turn freely.
   It is ADVISABLE to

   A. check each gear mesh for backlash
   B. connect the input shaft to a motor and run-in the gears
   C. completely disassemble the gearbox and replace all of the gears
   D. work the gears free with short blows from a babbit hammer

10. When lifting a heavy object, a maintainer should

    A. bend at the waist
    B. keep both feet together
    C. keep his back straight
    D. keep his arms extended

11. Assume that your foreman asks you to use a newly designed machine for resurfacing brake drums.
    Of the following, the information that your foreman would probably be MOST interested in obtaining from you would be the _____ the new machine.

    A. space requirements for
    B. power requirements for
    C. best maintenance procedure for
    D. increase in production obtained with

12. Hand taps for cutting threads are generally grouped in sets of three.
    In order to tap a thread to the bottom of a blind hole in a steel block, these taps are usually used in the following order: _____ tap.

    A. Plug tap, taper tap, bottoming
    B. Taper tap, plug tap, bottoming
    C. Taper tap, bottoming tap, plug
    D. Bottoming tap, taper tap, plug

13. A type of stone which is frequently used to sharpen tools is

    A. carborundum
    B. pumice
    C. sandstone
    D. soapstone

14. Gage blocks are used for checking the accuracy of

    A. manometers
    B. torque wrenches
    C. micrometers
    D. thermometers

15. In order to release a tapered shank drill from the drilling machine spindle, it is BEST to use a hammer and a drill

    A. bit
    B. center punch
    C. drift
    D. chuck

16. Repeated use of a machinist's hammer frequently results in uneven face wear.
    In order to recondition the face of the hammer, it would be BEST to use a(n)

    A. file
    B. grinder
    C. milling machine
    D. anvil

17. The BEST tool to use for cutting copper tubing with a .030 inch wall thickness is a   17._____

    A. sharp chisel
    B. hacksaw with a fine tooth blade
    C. coarse file
    D. pair of tin shears

18. The PRIMARY purpose of the spiral flutes on a twist drill is to   18._____

    A. carry the chips away from the point
    B. increase the cutting speed of the drill
    C. improve the accuracy of drilling
    D. prevent the drill from wandering off the center line

19. The reading on the 0 to 1 inch micrometer shown is MOST NEARLY   19._____

    A. 0.125
    B. 0.224
    C. 0.254
    D. 0.285

20. The BEST time to inspect grinding machine wheels for flaws is   20._____

    A. before starting the machine
    B. after the wheel has been dressed
    C. every three months
    D. at the end of each job

21. A chamfer is usually machined on the end of a piece of round bar stock before cutting threads on the bar stock. The PURPOSE of this chamfer is to   21._____

    A. carry the chips away from the die
    B. make the bar stiffer
    C. start the threads square with the center line
    D. protect the cutting edges of the cutting die

22. A multimeter or multitester is often used in troubleshooting of electrical problems. This type of instrument can measure _____ and voltage.   22._____

    A. wattage, current,
    B. inductance, capacitance,
    C. capacitance, resistance,
    D. current, resistance,

23. Assume that you are on your way to the locker room after completing your tour and you notice that oil has dripped onto the floor, creating a slipping hazard. You should   23._____

    A. call the location chief and tell him about it
    B. ignore it since it is not in your work area
    C. get some *speedi-dry* from a nearby supply and spread it over the oil
    D. wait until you return from the locker room to take care of it

24. All repair shop employees should develop good habits concerning safe work practices. In order to develop these good habits, it would be BEST for a maintainer continually to

    A. experiment with new methods and learn from his mistakes
    B. observe the other maintainers and do what everyone else does
    C. attend classroom lectures and write everything down
    D. listen to the instructions from his foreman and follow them

25. One common cause of accidents in the repair shop is that

    A. critical parts are kept locked in storage areas
    B. emergencies frequently require changes in work schedules
    C. certain tools are overhauled instead of being replaced regularly
    D. materials are left on the floor instead of in designated storage areas

---

KEY (CORRECT ANSWERS)

1. C	11. D
2. B	12. B
3. D	13. A
4. D	14. C
5. D	15. C
6. C	16. B
7. D	17. B
8. C	18. A
9. A	19. C
10. C	20. A

21. C
22. D
23. C
24. D
25. D

EXAMINATION SECTION
TEST 1

DIRECTIONS: Each question or incomplete statement is followed by several suggested answers or completions. Select the one that BEST answers the question or completes the statement. *PRINT THE LETTER OF THE CORRECT ANSWER IN THE SPACE AT THE RIGHT.*

Questions 1-8.

DIRECTIONS: Questions 1 through 8 involve tests on the fuse box arrangement shown below. All tests are to be performed with a neon tester or a lamp test bank consisting of two 6-watt, 120-volt lamps connected in series. Do not make any assumptions about the conditions of the circuits. Draw your conclusions only from the information obtained with the neon tester or the two-lamp test bank, applied to the circuits as called for.

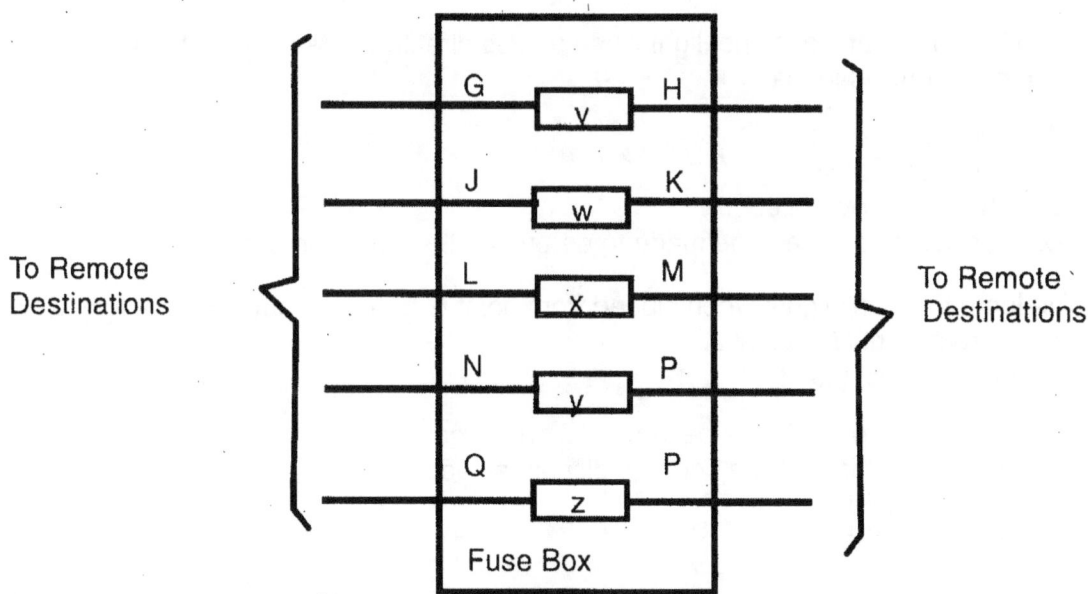

1. The two lamp test bank is placed from point G to joint J, and both lamps light. One of the lamps is momentarily removed from its socket; during that instant, the other lamp in the series-connected test bank should

   A. go dark
   B. get dimmer
   C. remain at same brightness
   D. get brighter

   1._____

2. The test bank with two 60-watt, 120-volt lamps in series should be used on circuits with

   A. wattages only from 60 to 120 watts
   B. wattages only from 0 to 120 watts
   C. voltages only from 120 to 240 volts
   D. voltages only from 0 to 240 volts

   2._____

39

3. The neon tester is placed from point G to point J and only one-half of the neon tester lights.
   It should be concluded that

   A. half of the tester has gone bad
   B. a wire has become disconnected in the circuit
   C. the voltage is AC
   D. the voltage is DC

4. If both lamps in the test bank light when placed directly across one of the above fuses, it should be concluded that

   A. the fuse is good
   B. the fuse is blown
   C. the fuse is overrated
   D. further tests have to be made to determine the condition of the fuse

5. If the lamp test bank does not light when placed directly across one of the above fuses, it should be concluded that

   A. the fuse is good
   B. the fuse is blown
   C. the fuse is overrated
   D. further tests have to be made to determine the condition of the fuse

6. The lamp test bank lights when placed from point G to point J but does not light when placed from point H to point J.
   It should be concluded that

   A. the wire to point H has become disconnected
   B. the wire to point J has become disconnected
   C. fuse v is bad
   D. fuse w is bad

7. The lamp test bank lights when placed from point L to point N but does not light when placed from point M to point P.
   It should be concluded that

   A. both fuses x and y are bad
   B. either fuse x or fuse y is bad or both are bad
   C. both fuses x and y are good
   D. these tests do not indicate the condition of any fuse

8. The lamp test bank is placed from point L to point N, then from N to point Q, and finally from point L to point Q. In each case, both lamps light to full brightness.
   It should be concluded that points L, N, and Q have

   A. three-phase, 120 volts, AC, line-to-line
   B. plus and minus 120 volts, DC
   C. three-phase, 208 volts, AC
   D. plus and minus 240 volts, DC

9. An automatic device used for regulating air temperature is a(n)

   A. rheostat   B. aquastat   C. thermostat   D. duostat

10. Assume that you have just completed a certain maintenance job which you feel is satisfactory, but your foreman asks you to make certain changes.
    The BEST procedure for you to follow is to

    A. request the foreman to assign this work to someone else
    B. have another maintainer verify that the job was done properly
    C. ask the foreman the reasons for the changes
    D. complain to the foreman's superior of this waste of time

11. The PROPER set of tools and equipment to be used to clean and adjust the ignition points of an automobile consists of a

    A. screwdriver, feeler gauge, and point file
    B. wrench, micrometer, and sandpaper
    C. scraper, micrometer, and emery cloth
    D. V-block, pliers, and sandpaper

12. The voltage developed in each cell of an automobile battery is _____ volts.

    A. 2   B. 4   C. 6   D. 12

13. The one of the following tools that is NOT used to clear plumbing stoppages is a

    A. force-cup   B. drain auger
    C. snake   D. pick-out iron

14. Eyebolts are generally fastened to the shells of machinery in order to

    A. act as a leveling device
    B. facilitate lifting
    C. permit easy tagging of the equipment
    D. reinforce the machine shells

15. When grinding a weld smooth, it is MOST important to avoid

    A. grinding too slowly
    B. overheating the surrounding metal
    C. grinding away too much of the weld
    D. grinding after the weld has cooled off

16. A cold chisel whose head has become *mushroomed* should NOT be used because

    A. it is impossible to hit the head squarely
    B. the chisel will not cut accurately
    C. chips might fly from the head
    D. the chisel has lost its *temper*

17. The type of screwdriver specially made to be used in tight spots is the

    A. Phillips   B. offset
    C. square shank   D. truss

18. An indication that a fluorescent lamp in a fixture should be replaced is

    A. humming in the fixture
    B. the ends of the lamp remain black when the lamp is lit
    C. poor or slow starting
    D. the lamp does not shut off each time the OFF button is pressed

19. Asbestos is used as a covering on electrical wires to provide protection from

    A. high voltage   B. high temperatures
    C. water damage   D. electrolysis

20. Many electric power tools, such as drills, have a third conductor in the line cord which should be connected to a grounded part of the power receptacle.
    The reason for this is to

    A. have a spare wire in case one power wire should break
    B. strengthen the power lead so that it cannot be easily damaged
    C. protect the user of the tool from electrical shocks
    D. allow use of the tool for extended periods of time without overheating

21. Employees are responsible for the good care, proper maintenance, and serviceable condition of the property issued or assigned for their use.
    As used above, *serviceable condition* means the property is in a state where it is

    A. capable of being repaired   B. easily handled
    C. fit for use   D. least expensive

22. A brush that has been used in shellac should be cleaned by washing it in

    A. water   B. linseed oil
    C. lacquer thinner   D. alcohol

23. Excessive moisture on a surface being painted would MOST likely result in

    A. alligatoring   B. blistering
    C. cracking   D. sagging

24. In order to reverse the direction of rotation of a series motor, the

    A. connections to the armature should be reversed
    B. connections to both the armature and the series field should be reversed
    C. connections of the motor to the power lines should be reversed
    D. series field should be placed in shunt with the armature

25. A megger is an instrument used to measure

    A. capacitance   B. insulation resistance
    C. power   D. illumination levels

26. The first aid treatment for chemical burns on the skin is

    A. treatment with ointment and then bandaging
    B. washing with large quantities of water and then treating as heat burns
    C. treatment with a neutralizing agent and no bandaging
    D. application of sodium bicarbonate and then bandaging

27. The chemical MOST frequently used to clean drains clogged with grease is 27.____

   A. muriatic acid B. soda ash
   C. ammonia D. caustic soda

28. When tapping a blind hole in a steel plate, the FIRST type of tap to use is a _____ tap. 28.____

   A. plug B. taper C. lead D. bottoming

29. A common handshaving tool used in woodwork is a(n) 29.____

   A. trammel B. router C. auger D. plane

30. *Dressing* a grinding wheel refers to 30.____

   A. making the wheel thinner
   B. replacing with a new wheel
   C. repairing a crack in the wheel
   D. making the wheel round

31. The maintainer who is MOST valuable is the one who 31.____

   A. offers to do the heavy lifting
   B. asks many questions about the work
   C. listens to instructions and carries them out
   D. makes many suggestions on work procedures

32. Of the following, turpentine is used for thinning 32.____

   A. latex paint B. red lead paint
   C. calcimine D. shellac

33. Of the following, the hacksaw blade BEST suited for cutting thin-walled tubing is one which has _____ teeth/inch. 33.____

   A. 14 B. 18 C. 24 D. 32

34. Because of its weather-resistant properties, a varnish commonly used on exterior surfaces is _____ varnish. 34.____

   A. spar B. flat C. rubbing D. hard oil

35. A trip spring or spring cylinder on a snow plow assembly is a device that 35.____

   A. absorbs the shock of impact when the plow strikes an obstacle in the road
   B. provides for snap-action in the lowering of the plow blade
   C. allows for quick removal or attachment of the snow plow supporting frame
   D. detaches the plow blade and lets it hang free when the plow blade is dragged backwards

36. The term *preventative maintenance* is used to identify a plan whereby 36.____

   A. equipment is serviced according to a regular schedule
   B. equipment is serviced as soon as it fails
   C. equipment is replaced as soon as it becomes obsolete
   D. all equipment is replaced periodically

37. The ratio of air to gasoline in an automobile engine is controlled by the

   A. gas filter
   B. fuel pump
   C. carburetor
   D. intake manifold

38. *Energizer* is another name given to the

   A. automobile battery
   B. fluorescent fixture ballast
   C. battery charger
   D. generator shunt field

39. Wearshoes may be found on

   A. circuit breakers
   B. automobile brake systems
   C. snow plows
   D. door sills

40. When moving heavy equipment by means of pipe rollers, it is MOST important to

   A. use solid steel rollers
   B. use rollers with different diameters
   C. see that the trailing roller does not slip out from under the equipment
   D. use more than three rollers at all times

41. The one of the following storage areas that is BEST for the storage of paint is one which is

   A. unheated and not ventilated
   B. cool and ventilated
   C. sunny and ventilated
   D. warm and not ventilated

42. The leverage that can be obtained with a wrench is determined mainly by the

   A. material of which the wrench is made
   B. gripping surface of the jaw
   C. length of the handle
   D. thickness of the wrench

43. A star drill is used to bore holes in

   A. steel   B. concrete   C. wood   D. sheet metal

44. The one of the following actions of a maintainer that is MOST likely to contribute to a good working relationship between him and his assistant is for him to

   A. observe the same rules of conduct that he expects his assistant to observe
   B. freely give advice on his assistant's personal problems
   C. always be frank and outspoken to his assistant in pointing out his faults
   D. expect his assistant to perform with equal efficiency on any job assigned

45. Three common types of windows are

   A. batten, casement, and awning
   B. batten, casement, and double-hung
   C. batten, double-hung, and awning
   D. casement, double-hung, and awning

46. A staircase has twelve risers, each 6 3/4" high. The TOTAL rise of the staircase is

    A. $6'2\frac{1}{4}"$ B. 6'9"   C. 7'0"   D. 7'3 3/4"

47. A twenty-foot straight ladder placed at an angle against a wall should be at a distance from the wall equal to _____ feet.

    A. 3   B. 5   C. 7   D. 9

48. Reflective sheeting traffic signs that have become dirty should be wiped with kerosene or gasoline FOLLOWED by a

    A. wiping with a soft cloth soaked in thin oil
    B. hand rub with very fine sandpaper
    C. wash with detergent and a rinse with water
    D. coating of shellac applied with a brush

49. A temporary wooden fence carrying red flags and built around an opening in a pavement to warn oncoming traffic is known as a

    A. batter board   B. bulkhead
    C. bollard   D. barricade

50. *Four-ply belted* is used to describe the construction of

    A. belt-drive pulleys
    B. auto tires
    C. electrical wiring insulation
    D. seat belts

KEY (CORRECT ANSWERS)

1. A	11. A	21. C	31. C	41. B
2. D	12. A	22. D	32. B	42. C
3. D	13. D	23. B	33. D	43. B
4. B	14. B	24. A	34. A	44. A
5. D	15. C	25. B	35. A	45. D
6. C	16. C	26. B	36. A	46. B
7. B	17. B	27. D	37. C	47. B
8. C	18. B	28. B	38. A	48. C
9. C	19. B	29. D	39. C	49. D
10. C	20. C	30. D	40. C	50. B

TEST 2

DIRECTIONS: Each question or incomplete statement is followed by several suggested answers or completions. Select the one that BEST answers the question or completes the statement. *PRINT THE LETTER OF THE CORRECT ANSWER IN THE SPACE AT THE RIGHT.*

1. An oil bath filter is MOST often used on a(n)

    A. air compressor B. auto engine
    C. electric generator D. steam boiler

2. A 3-ohm resistor placed across a 12-volt battery will dissipate _____ watts.

    A. 3   B. 4   C. 12   D. 48

3. Instead of using fuses, modern electric wiring uses

    A. quick switches B. circuit breakers
    C. fusible links D. lag blocks

4. The MOST common combination of gases used for welding is

    A. carbon dioxide and acetylene
    B. nitrogen and hydrogen
    C. oxygen and acetylene
    D. oxygen and hydrogen

5. If a wheel has turned through an angle of 180, then it has made _____ revolution(s).

    A. 1/4   B. 1/2   C. 1/8   D. 18

6. Sewer gas is prevented from backing up through a plumbing fixture by a

    A. water trap B. return elbow
    C. check valve D. float valve

7. Putty that is too stiff is made workable by adding

    A. gasoline B. linseed oil
    C. water D. lacquer thinner

8. A vertical wood member in the wall of a wood frame house is known as a

    A. A stringer B. ridge member
    C. stud D. header

9. A 10-to-1 step-down transformer has an input of 1 ampere at 120 volts AC. If the losses are negligible, the output of the transformer is _____ volts.

    A. 1 ampere at 12 B. .1 ampere at 1200
    C. 10 amperes at 12 D. 10 amperes at 120

10. An oscilloscope is an instrument used in

    A. measuring noise levels
    B. displaying waveforms of electrical signals
    C. indicating the concentrations of pollutants in air
    D. photographing high-speed events

11. Assume that a brake pedal of a truck goes to the floorboard when depressed. The one of the following that could cause this condition is

    A. a leak in the hydraulic lines
    B. a clogged hydraulic line
    C. scored drums
    D. glazed linings

12. The universal joints of an automobile are located on the

    A. suspension springs
    B. steering linkages
    C. wheel cylinders
    D. drive shaft

13. The MAIN purpose of a flexible coupling is to connect two shafts which are

    A. of different diameters
    B. of different shapes
    C. not in exact alignment
    D. of different material

14. When using a standard measuring micrometer, starting with a zero reading, one complete counterclockwise revolution of the sleeve will give a reading of _____ inch.

    A. .001   B. .010   C. .025   D. .250

15. If a nut is to be tightened to an exact specified value of inch-lbs., the wrench to use is a _____ wrench.

    A. spanner   B. box   C. lock-jaw   D. torque

16. Common permanent type anti-freezes for automobile cooling systems are MAINLY

    A. alcohol
    B. methanol
    C. ethylene glycol
    D. trychloroethylene

17. Plexiglas is also called

    A. mylar   B. lucite   C. isinglass   D. PVC

18. Long, curved lines are BEST cut in 1/4" plexiglas with a _____ saw.

    A. rip   B. jig   C. keyhole   D. coping

19. The specific gravity of storage battery cells can be measured with a(n)

    A. odometer   B. hydrometer   C. ammeter   D. dwell meter

20. A nail set is a tool used for

    A. straightening bent nails
    B. measuring nail sizes
    C. cutting nails to specified size
    D. driving a nail head into wood

21. To cut a number of 2" x 4" lengths of wood accurately at an angle of 45°, it is BEST to use a

    A. protractor   B. mitre-box   C. triangle   D. square

22. The type of fastener MOST commonly used when bolting to concrete uses a(n)
    A. expansion shield   B. U-bolt
    C. toggle bolt   D. turnbuckle

23. When an automobile engine does not start on a damp day, the trouble is MOST likely in the _____ system.
    A. ignition   B. cooling   C. fuel   D. lubricating

24. The battery of an automobile is prevented from discharging back through the alternator by the blocking action of the
    A. commutator   B. diodes   C. brushes   D. slip rings

25. The master cylinder in an automobile is actuated by the
    A. steering column   B. brake pedal
    C. clutch plate   D. cam shaft

26. The FINEST sandpaper from among the following is No.
    A. 3   B. 1   C. 2/0   D. 6/0

27. A screw whose head is buried below the surface of the wood that it is screwed into is said to be
    A. countersunk   B. scalloped
    C. expanded   D. flushed

28. The one of the following devices which is used to measure angles is the
    A. caliper   B. protractor
    C. marking gauge   D. divider

29. Before a new oil stone is used, it should be
    A. heated   B. soaked in oil
    C. coated with shellac   D. washed with soapy water

30. Dies are used for
    A. threading the outside ends of metal pipes
    B. making sweated joints on lead pipes
    C. cutting nipples to exact lengths
    D. caulking cast-iron pipe joints

31. The energy stored by a storage battery is commonly given in
    A. volts   B. amperes
    C. ampere-hours   D. kilowatts

32. *Vapor lock* occurs in automobile
    A. gas tanks   B. crankcases
    C. transmissions   D. carburetors

33. A woodworking tool used to bore odd-size holes for which there is no standard auger bit is a(n)

   A. single twist auger
   B. double twist auger
   C. expansive bit
   D. straight fluted drill

33.____

34. Soap is sometimes applied to wood screws in order to

   A. prevent rust
   B. make a tight fit
   C. make insertion easier
   D. prevent wood splitting

34.____

35. On a long run of copper tubing, the tubing is often bent in the shape of a horseshoe rather than being run in a straight line.
The MAIN reason for this is to

   A. allow an excess that could be used in future repairs
   B. make it easier to install the tubing
   C. permit the tubing to expand and contract with changes in temperature
   D. eliminate the need for accurate measurements in cutting the tubing

35.____

36. Loss of seal water in a house water trap is prevented by the use of a

   A. drainage tee   B. faucet   C. hose bibb   D. vent

36.____

37. BX is a designation for a type of

   A. flexible armored electric cable
   B. flexible gas line
   C. rigid conduit
   D. electrical insulation

37.____

38. *WYE-WYE* and *DELTA-WYE* are two

   A. types of DC motor windings
   B. arrangements of 3-phase transformer connections
   C. types of electrical splices
   D. shapes of commutator bars

38.____

39. Green lumber should NOT be used in the building of scaffolding because it

   A. will not hold nails well
   B. easily splits when nailed
   C. may warp on drying
   D. is too expensive

39.____

40. *Scotchlite* ready-made traffic sign faces with heat-activated adhesive backings are applied to backing blanks by use of a

   A. temperature-controlled oven
   B. vacuum applicator
   C. hot water bath
   D. heated roller assembly

40.____

41. *Scotchcal* is a(n)

   A. reflective sheeting
   B. epoxy protective paint
   C. fluorescent film
   D. high temperature lubricant

41.____

42. Wooden ladders should NOT be painted because the paint

    A. is inflammable
    B. may cover defects in the wood
    C. makes the rungs slippery
    D. may deteriorate the wood

43. To prevent ladders from slipping, the bottoms of the ladder side rails are OFTEN fitted with

    A. automatic locks   B. ladder shoes
    C. ladder hooks   D. stirrups

44. A bowline is

    A. the sag that a scaffold develops when men get on it
    B. a knot with a loop that does not run
    C. a temporary telephone wire strung during emergencies
    D. the reference line established in ditch excavations

45. A method sometimes used to prevent a pipe from buckling during a bending operation is to

    A. bend the pipe very quickly
    B. keep the seam of the pipe on the outside of the bend
    C. nick the pipe at the center of the bend
    D. pack the inside of the pipe with sand

46. A rectifier changes

    A. DC to AC
    B. AC to DC
    C. single-phase power to three-phase power
    D. battery power to three-phase power

47. Continuity in a de-energized electrical circuit may be checked with a(n)

    A. voltmeter   B. ohmmeter   C. neon tester   D. rheostat

48. Of the following crankcase oils, the one that should be used in sub-zero weather is SAE

    A. 10W   B. 20W   C. 20   D. 30

49. Caster in an automobile is an adjustment in the

    A. ignition system   B. drive-shaft
    C. rear differential   D. front suspension

50. If the spark plugs in an engine run too hot, the result is MOST likely that

    A. oil and carbon compounds will accumulate on the insulators
    B. the electrodes will wear rapidly
    C. the timing will be retarded
    D. the ignition coil may become damaged

KEY (CORRECT ANSWERS)

1. B	11. A	21. B	31. C	41. C
2. B	12. D	22. A	32. D	42. B
3. B	13. C	23. A	33. C	43. B
4. C	14. C	24. B	34. C	44. B
5. B	15. D	25. B	35. C	45. D
6. A	16. C	26. D	36. D	46. B
7. B	17. B	27. A	37. A	47. B
8. C	18. B	28. B	38. B	48. A
9. C	19. B	29. B	39. C	49. D
10. B	20. D	30. A	40. B	50. B

EXAMINATION SECTION
TEST 1

DIRECTIONS: Each question or incomplete statement is followed by several suggested answers or completions. Select the one that BEST answers the question or completes the statement. *PRINT THE LETTEE OF THE CORRECT ANSWER IN THE SPACE AT THE RIGHT.*

1. Of the following, the type of welding in which a filler rod is COMMONLY used is   1._____

   A. resistance   B. carbon arc   C. spot   D. pressure

2. A small short bead used as a temporary fastener is known as a(n) _____ weld.   2._____

   A. spot   B. edge   C. plug   D. tack

3. The one of the following which is the MOST important reason for using the step-back method of welding is to   3._____

   A. increase the strength of the weld
   B. speed the process of welding
   C. reduce the amount of warping
   D. decrease formation of slag

4. In butt welds, the purpose of open roots is to   4._____

   A. reduce the amount of electrode required
   B. secure more overlap
   C. aid slag formation
   D. obtain better penetration

5. Stresses in a welded piece may be relieved by   5._____

   A. annealing   B. case hardening
   C. cold drawing   D. quenching

6. Brazing is MOST commonly done at tempera.tures ranging from *approximately*   6._____

   A. 300° to 900° F   B. 1100° to 2000° F
   C. 2300° to 3000° F   D. 3300° to 3800° F

7. Bronze welding is MOST commonly used for welding   7._____

   A. wrought iron   B. aluminum
   C. white metal   D. chrome steel

Questions 8-11.

DIRECTIONS: In Questions 8 to 11, inclusive, there are shown in Column I various welding symbols. Column II gives types of welds. For each symbol listed in Column I, enter in the appropriate space on the right the capital letter in front of the type of weld listed in Column II which the symbol illustrates.

COLUMN I	COLUMN II
8. ⌒	A. flush
	B. plug
	C. weld all around
9. |	D. square
	E. bevel
	F. fillet
	G. bead
10. ◺	
11. ○	

12. The one of the following which indicates an intermittent weld is

    A. [symbol]   B. [symbol]   C. [symbol]   D. [symbol]

13. The throat of a 1/2 inch fillet weld is MOST NEARLY _____ inches.

    A. .25   B. .35   C. .45   D. .55

14. Spelter is MOST commonly used in

    A. electric arc welding   B. oxy-acetylene fusion welding
    C. brazing   D. quenching

15. If one dozen 1/8" welding rods cost 48 cents, 37 rods would cost

    A. $1.44   B. $1.48   C. $1.52   D. $1.56

16. The sum of the following numbers, 6 5/8, 3 3/4, 4 1/2, 5 1/8, is

    A. 19 3/4   B. 19 7/8   C. 20   D. 20 1/8

17. Of the following, the one that is a method used to test completed welds is

    A. soaking bath   B. electrolytic resistance
    C. photo-elastic strain   D. acid-etch

18. Of the following, the term that defines a defect in a weld is

    A. scarf   B. tuyere   C. cold shut   D. cohesion

19. When clean steel is heated to a faint straw color, the temperature of the steel, based upon this color, is APPROXIMATELY

    A. 400° F   B. 600° F   C. 800° F   D. 1000° F

20. Of the following metals, the one that has a fibrous structure is 20.____

    A. gray cast iron B. manganese steel
    C. low carbon steel D. wrought iron

21. Of the following alloying elements, the one that is MOST commonly used in tool steel is 21.____

    A. manganese B. zirconium C. titanium D. tungsten

22. Of the following automotive parts, the one for which welding of any type would be LEAST desirable is 22.____

    A. crankcase B. crankshaft
    C. cylinder block D. body

23. Of the following metals, the one that is MOST commonly *hard-faced* is 23.____

    A. aluminum B. bronze
    C. monel D. high speed steel

24. Studs are frequently used to strengthen the welds in 24.____

    A. iron castings B. structural steel
    C. bronze bushings D. tool steel

25. Incomplete penetration in a weld is MOST likely to be caused by too 25.____

    A. rigid a joint B. large a welding rod
    C. large a welding tip D. slow a welding speed

26. Of the following, the metal with the LOWEST melting point is 26.____

    A. aluminum B. bronze C. monel D. cast iron

27. Quenching to harden steel is MOST commonly done in a bath of 27.____

    A. lye B. soda-ash C. brine D. muriatic acid

28. Shrinkage due to welding in non-preheated pieces can be reduced by 28.____

    A. open roots B. peening
    C. large welds D. increased number of welds

29. Brazing is MOST commonly used on 29.____

    A. lead B. bronze C. babbit D. aluminum

30. Impact resisting pads on all types of machinery are MOST frequently made of 30.____

    A. monel B. aluminum C. bronze D. inconel

31. Drag is usually determined in relation to the consumption of 31.____

    A. oxygen B. acetylene C. rod D. power

Questions 32-35.

DIRECTIONS: Questions 32 to 35, inclusive, refer to the paragraph below. These questions are to be answered in strict accordance with the material in this paragraph.

Welds in sheet metal up to 1/16 inch in thickness can be made satisfactorily by flanging the edges of the joint. The edges are prepared by turning up a very thin lip or flange along the line of the joint. The height of this flange should be equal to the thickness of the sheet being welded. The edges should be alined so that the flanges stand up, and the joint should be tack-welded every 5 or 6 inches. Heavy angles or bars should be clamped on each side of the joint to prevent distortion or buckling. No filler metal is required for making this joint. The raised edges are quickly melted by the heat of the welding flame so as to produce an even weld bead which is nearly flush with the original sheet metal surface. By controlling the speed of welding and the motion of the flame, good fusion to the underside of the sheets can be obtained without burning through.

32. According to the above paragraph, satisfactory welds may be made in sheet metal by flanging the edges.
    The MAXIMUM thickness of metal recommended is

    A. 20 gauge B. 18 gauge C. 1/16" D. 5/64"

33. According to the above paragraph, good fusion may be obtained without burning through of the metal by controlling the motion of the flame and the

    A. size of tip   B. speed of welding
    C. oxygen flow   D. acetylene flow

34. According to the above paragraph, if the thickness of the metal is 1/32", then the flange height should be

    A. 1/64" B. 1/32" C. 1/16" D. 1/8"

35. According to the above paragraph, distortion in the welding of sheet metal may be prevented by

    A. controlling the speed of welding
    B. use of a flange of correct height
    C. use of proper filler metal
    D. clamping angles on each side of the joint

32. __
33. __
34. __
35. __

KEY (CORRECT ANSWERS)

1.	B	16.	C
2.	D	17.	D
3.	C	18.	C
4.	D	19.	A
5.	A	20.	D
6.	B	21.	D
7.	A	22.	B
8.	G	23.	C
9.	D	24.	A
10.	F	25.	B
11.	C	26.	A
12.	D	27.	C
13.	B	28.	B
14.	C	29.	B
15.	B	30.	C

31.	A
32.	C
33.	B
34.	B
35.	D

TEST 2

DIRECTIONS: Each question or incomplete statement is followed by several suggested answers or completions. Select the one that BEST answers the question or completes the statement. *PRINT THE LETTER OF THE CORRECT ANSWER IN THE SPACE AT THE RIGHT.*

Questions 1-4.

DIRECTIONS: Questions 1 through 4, inclusive, refer to the jig for testing welded specimens shown below. The jig is to be built up from plate by welding.

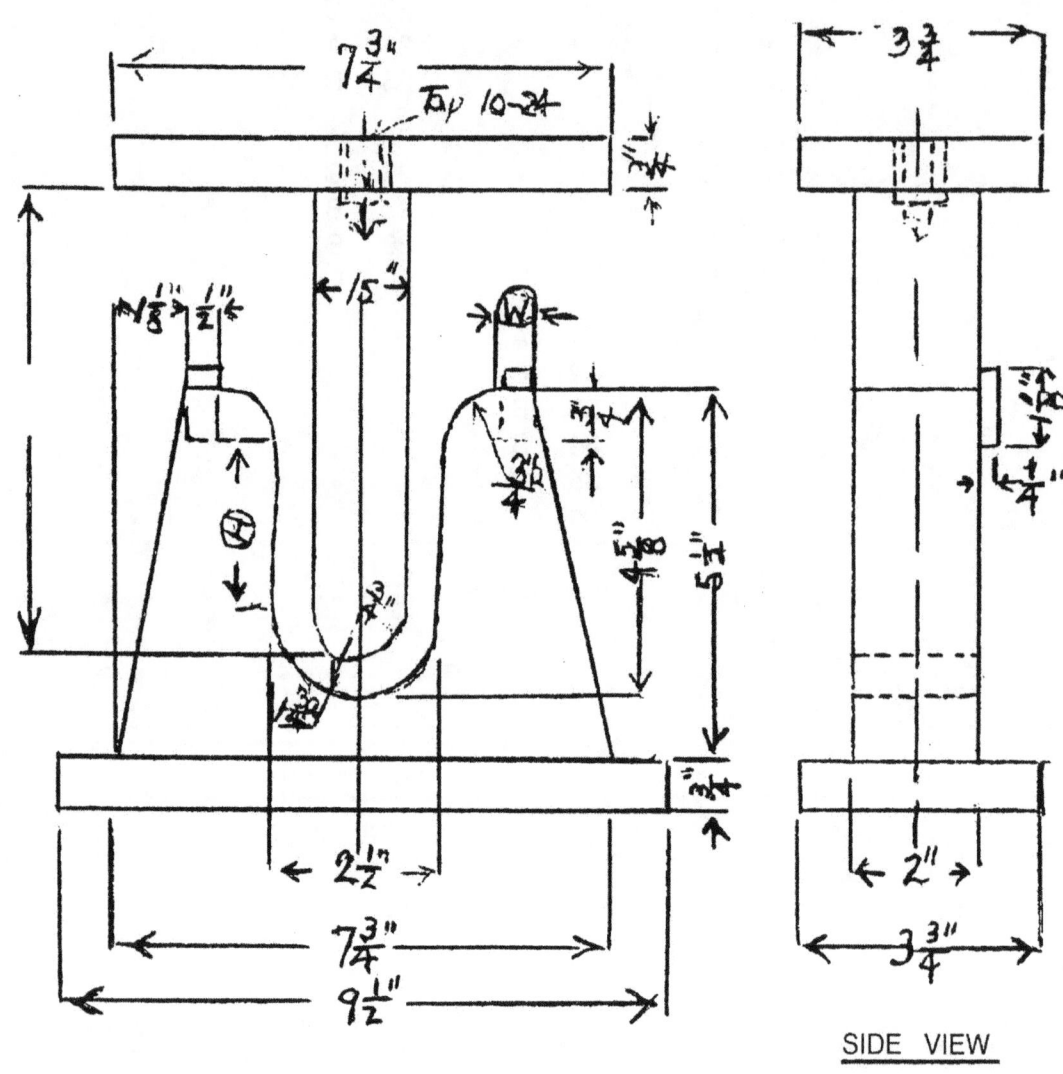

FRONT VIEW

SIDE VIEW

1. The type of weld that would MOST probably be used to weld the plates together is 1.____

   A. V bevel   B. U groove   C. plug   D. fillet

2. The symbol *Tap 10-24* at the top of the jig means that the hole is 2.____

   A. reamed   B. broached   C. threaded   D. punched

3. The length of the straight portion of the jig indicated by the letter *H* is

   A. 2 3/8"   B. 2 1/2"   C. 2 5/8"   D. 2 3/4"

4. The length of the straight portion of the jig indicated by the letter *W* is

   A. 3/4"   B. 7/8"   C. 1"   D. 1 1/8"

Questions 5-21.

DIRECTIONS: Questions 5 through 21, inclusive, are to be answered on the basis of welding with an electric arc welder.

5. Of the following, the MINIMUM voltage necessary to strike an arc with an alternating current machine is, in volts,

   A. 20   B. 40   C. 100   D. 140

6. According to the rules of the Department of Water Supply, Gas and Electricity, the MAXIMUM length of flexible cord or cable permitted for supplying current to a portable welder is _____ feet.

   A. 10   B. 20   C. 30   D. 40

7. The MINIMUM voltage required to strike an arc with a direct current welder is

   A. less than that required for an alternating current welder
   B. more than that required for an alternating current welder
   C. the same as that required for an alternating current welder
   D. more or less than that required for an alternating current welder depending on the type of electrode

8. Of the following, the one that would be MOST likely to appear on the name plate of an arc welder would be

   A. temperature of arc   B. number of feeders
   C. voltage   D. frequency

9. Splattering of the weld is caused by

   A. excessive current   B. too little current
   C. improper flux   D. lack of preheat

10. For a given voltage and current setting on an electric arc welder, decreasing the length of the arc

    A. increases the penetration
    B. decreases the penetration
    C. has no effect on the penetration
    D. may increase or decrease the penetration, depending on the voltage-current setting

11. For a given voltage and current setting on an electric arc welder, when the arc length is shortened, the arc voltage   11.____

   A. increases
   B. decreases
   C. stays constant
   D. may increase or decrease, depending on the electrode being used

12. Welding of light gauge metals requires _____ electrodes and _____ voltages.   12.____

   A. large; high
   B. large; low
   C. small; high
   D. small; low

13. In straight polarity,   13.____

   A. both the electrode and the work are negative
   B. both the electrode and the work are positive
   C. the electrode is negative, the work is positive
   D. the electrode is positive, the work is negative

14. Freezing of the electrode is caused by   14.____

   A. insufficient current
   B. electrode being held too long in contact with the work
   C. work not being clean
   D. improper electrode for work being done

15. When welding metal of the same thickness with the same electrode, in the overhead and in the flat position, welding in the overhead position USUALLY requires   15.____

   A. less voltage than the flat position
   B. more voltage than the flat position
   C. the same voltage as the flat position
   D. more or less voltage than the flat position depending on the metal being welded

16. Compared with a bare electrode, a shielded electrode produces   16.____

   A. more nitrides
   B. more oxidation
   C. a hotter arc
   D. a more stable arc

17. Arc blow is MOST commonly corrected by   17.____

   A. welding away from the ground
   B. changing the polarity of the electrode
   C. increasing the voltage
   D. decreasing the current

18. Preheating is MOST commonly used when welding   18.____

   A. high manganese-cast steel
   B. chrome-nickel stainless steel
   C. wrought iron
   D. bronze

19. When welding with a shielded electrode, the slag formed

    A. increases the rate of cooling of weld metal
    B. helps prevent warping
    C. slows the speed of welding
    D. removes oxides from the weld

20. When welding with an electric arc, you find that the arc has a hissing and steady sputtering sound.
    The MOST probable cause of this is

    A. low voltage   B. low current
    C. high voltage   D. high current

21. When welding in the flat position with 3/8" bare electrodes, the *approximate* range of amperes that would be used is MOST NEARLY

    A. 40 to 60   B. 110 to 150   C. 250 to 300   D. 450 to 550

Questions 22-35.

DIRECTIONS: Questions 22 through 35, inclusive, are to be answered on the basis of welding with an oxy-acetylene flame.

22. The color of the hose used to connect the torch to the acetylene cylinder is

    A. green   B. yellow   C. red   D. black

23. The tool MOST commonly used to clean a torch tip is a

    A. drill   B. file   C. scriber   D. reamer

24. To test for leaks in an oxy-acetylene torch, you should use

    A. a match   B. #6 fuel oil
    C. soapy water   D. carbon tetrachloride

25. Of the following statements relative to oxygen or acetylene cylinders, the one that is MOST NEARLY CORRECT is:

    A. Oxygen may be used in place of compressed air in compressed air equipment
    B. A wrench should not be used to open an oxygen cylinder valve
    C. A frozen acetylene cylinder valve should be thawed with boiling water
    D. Oxygen cylinders should be stored lying down

26. Acetylene is USUALLY used at a pressure of less than _____ lbs./sq.in.

    A. 15   B. 30   C. 45   D. 60

27. The hottest part of a neutral oxy-acetylene flame is located APPROXIMATELY

    A. at the outermost tip of the flame
    B. midway between the tip of the flame and the tip of the inner cone
    C. at the tip of the inner cone
    D. at the tip of the torch

28. The number of distinct flame zones in a reducing flame is 28.____

    A. 1   B. 2   C. 3   D. 4

29. A reducing flame has 29.____

    A. more oxygen by volume than acetylene
    B. more acetylene by volume than oxygen
    C. the same volume of oxygen and acetylene
    D. no acetylene

30. Fusion welding of cast steel is MOST commonly done with a(n) _____ flame. 30.____

    A. neutral   B. oxidizing   C. reducing   D. carburizing

31. When welding materials of the same thickness, the one of the following that requires the SMALLEST torch tip is 31.____

    A. cast iron   B. steel
    C. wrought iron   D. aluminum

32. As compared to fusion welding, brazing of the same thickness of steel requires 32.____

    A. a smaller torch tip
    B. a larger torch tip
    C. the same size torch tip
    D. a smaller or larger torch tip depending on the carbon content of the steel

33. Of the following statements relative to hard surfacing, the one that is MOST NEARLY CORRECT is: 33.____

    A. Alloys in hard surfacing rods will not oxidize if a neutral flame is used
    B. A smaller torch tip is used for hard surfacing than is used for fusion welding of steel of the same thickness
    C. Hard surfacing rods are least likely to be used when the part must be heat treated after welding
    D. Hard surfacing is usually done with a rod having a low Rockwell C test

34. Of the following metals to be fusion welded, the one for which a flux is USUALLY used is _____ steel. 34.____

    A. low carbon   B. stainless
    C. carbon-molybdenum   D. nickel alloy

35. A metal, when melted with an oxy-acetylene torch, gives off sparks. This metal MOST likely is 35.____

    A. gray cast iron   B. cast steel
    C. aluminum   D. monel

KEY (CORRECT ANSWERS)

1.	D	16.	D
2.	C	17.	A
3.	C	18.	D
4.	A	19.	D
5.	C	20.	A
6.	D	21.	D
7.	A	22.	C
8.	D	23.	A
9.	A	24.	C
10.	D	25.	B
11.	B	26.	A
12.	C	27.	C
13.	C	28.	C
14.	B	29.	B
15.	A	30.	A

31. D
32. A
33. C
34. B
35. B

EXAMINATION SECTION
TEST 1

DIRECTIONS: Each question or incomplete statement is followed by several suggested answers or completions. Select the one that BEST answers the question or completes the statement. *PRINT THE LETTER OF THE COREECT ANSWER IN THE SPACE AT THE RIGHT.*

Questions 1-4.

DIRECTIONS: Questions 1 through 4, inclusive, are based on the sketch of metal sheet shown below. (Sketch not to scale.)

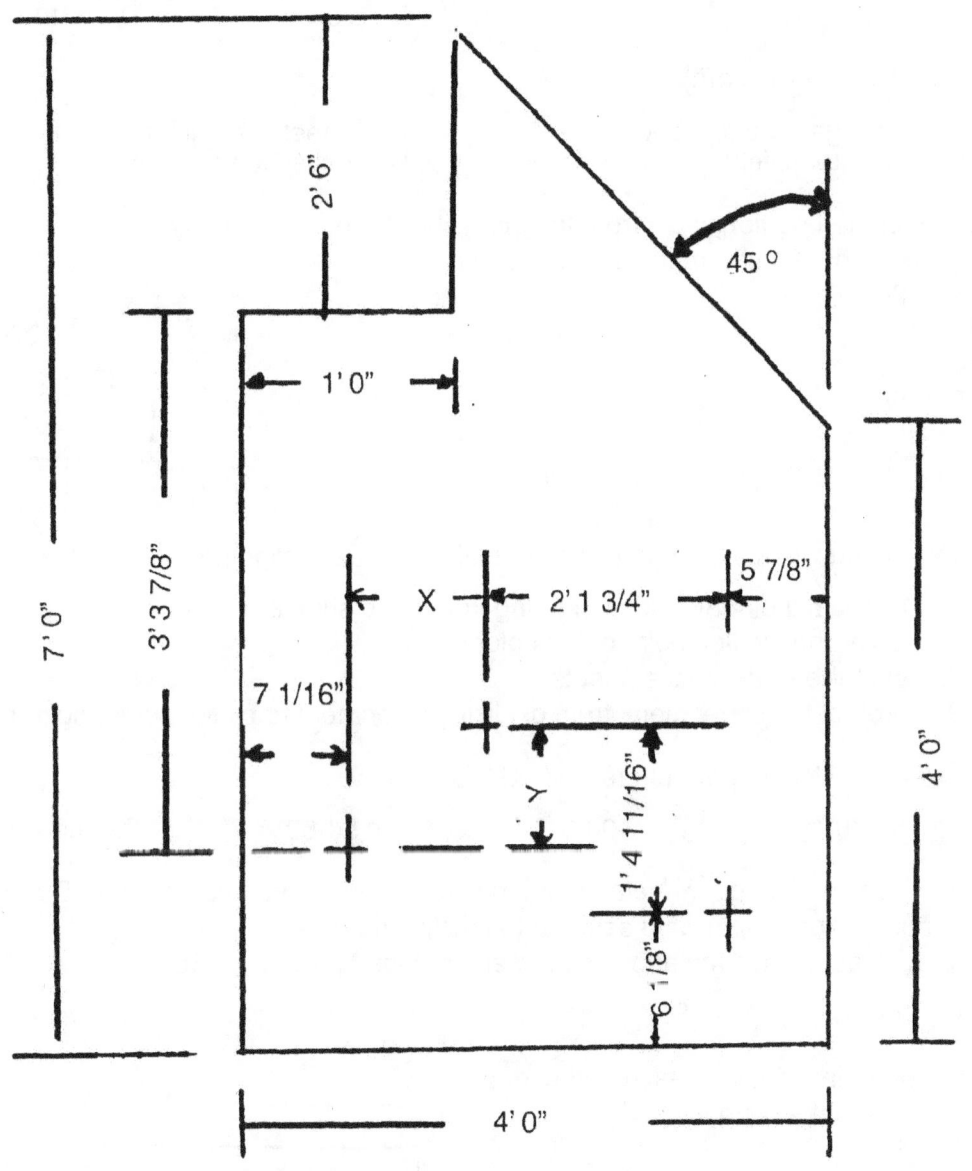

1. From the above sketch, the distance marked X is MOST NEARLY

   A. 5 1/4"   B. 6 5/16"   C. 7 1/8"   D. 9 5/16"

2. From the above sketch, the distance marked Y is MOST NEARLY

   A. 5 11/16"   B. 6 3/16"   C. 7 5/16"   D. 8 11/16"

3. In reference to the above sketch, if each piece is made from a rectangular piece of metal measuring 4' x 7', the percent of waste material is MOST NEARLY

   A. 10%   B. 15%   C. 25%   D. 30%

4. In reference to the above sketch, if the metal is 1/4" thick and weighs 144 pounds per cubic foot, the net weight of one piece would be MOST NEARLY _____ pounds.

   A. 51   B. 63   C. 75   D. 749

5. A *Pittsburgh lock* is a(n)

   A. emergency door lock   B. sheet metal joint
   C. elevator safety   D. boiler valve

6. If the shaded portion is cut from the plate shown, the area (in square inches) of the remaining portion is

   A. 26
   B. 29
   C. 32
   D. 58

7. Flux is used when soldering two pieces of sheet metal together in order to

   A. conduct the heat of the soldering iron to the sheets
   B. lower the melting point of the solder
   C. glue the solder to the sheets
   D. protect the sheet metal from oxidizing when heated by the soldering iron

8. Solder used for copper gutters is MOST frequently

   A. 30-70   B. 40-60   C. 50-50   D. 60-40

9. Specifications for hollow metal doors to be used on a construction state: Double door without mullions. Spot weld astragal to inactive door.
   Astragal, as used in the above statement, means MOST NEARLY

   A. louver   B. hinge   C. molding   D. veneer

10. The width, in inches, of each of the identical slots in the plate is

    A. 1/4
    B. 3/16
    C. 1/8
    D. 1/16

11. Metal gutters are MOST commonly made of

   A. stainless steel B. copper
   C. monel metal D. brass

12. The type of seam GENERALLY used in the construction of sheet metal cylinders of small diameters is the _____ seam.

   A. double-edged B. folded
   C. double-hemmed D. simple lap

13. With respect to soldering, it is LEAST important that

   A. the soldering copper be clean and well-tinned
   B. a good flux suitable for the metal being soldered be used
   C. the joint to be soldered be well-cleaned
   D. a lot of solder be used

14. When two sheet metal plates are riveted together, a specified minimum distance must be provided from the edge of each plate to the nearest line of rivets in order to prevent

   A. the rivet heads from working loose
   B. the rivets from being sheared
   C. tearing of the material between the rivets and the edges of the plates
   D. excessive stress on the rivets

15. It is BEST to cut a piece of sheet metal with a pair of snips by starting each cut with the metal sheet

   A. out near the points of the snips
   B. as far back in the jaws as possible
   C. midway between the snip points and the pivot
   D. one-quarter the way between the snip points and the pivot

16. A sheet metal plate has been cut in the form of a right triangle with sides of 5, 12, and 13 inches.
    The area of this plate, in square inches, is

   A. 30 B. 32 1/2 C. 60 D. 78

17. To form the head of a tinner's rivet, the PROPER tool to use is a rivet

   A. anvil B. plate C. set D. brake

18. The area of the metal plate shown at the right, minus the hole area, is MOST NEARLY _____ square inches.

   A. 8.5
   B. 8.9
   C. 9.4
   D. 10.1

19.

The center punch is numbered

A. 1   B. 2   C. 3   D. 4

20. Leather gloves should be worn when handling sheet metal PRIMARILY because

    A. pressure on the metal might cause it to bend
    B. the edges and corners of the metal may be sharp
    C. natural oil or moisture from hands corrodes the metal
    D. leather provides a more secure grip

21. A type of rivet which can be put in place even when a worker does NOT have access to the back side of the work is known as a _____ rivet.

    A. bucking   B. double-head
    C. pop   D. side

22. The open-top tin box shown at the right can be made by bending along the dotted lines of the flat cut sheet marked

A.   B.   C.   D.

23. The BEST flux to use when soldering galvanized iron is

    A. killed acid   B. sal-ammoniac
    C. muriatic acid   D. resin

24. When soldering a vertical joint, the soldering iron should be tinned on _____ side(s).

    A. one   B. two   C. three   D. four

25. The thickness of a sheet of 16-ounce copper is MOST NEARLY _____ inch.

    A. 1/50   B. 1/30   C. 1/20   D. 1/8

KEY (CORRECT ANSWERS)

1. D
2. D
3. C
4. B
5. B

6. C
7. D
8. C
9. C
10. C

11. B
12. D
13. D
14. C
15. B

16. A
17. C
18. B
19. A
20. B

21. C
22. D
23. C
24. A
25. A

TEST 2

DIRECTIONS: Each question or incomplete statement is followed by several suggested answers or completions. Select the one that BEST answers the question or completes the statement. *PRINT THE LETTER OF THE CORRECT ANSWER IN THE SPACE AT THE RIGHT.*

1. When drilling a small hole in sheet copper, the BEST practice is to   1.____

   A. make a dent with a center punch first
   B. put some cutting oil at the point you intend to drill
   C. use a slow speed drill to prevent overheating
   D. use an auger type bit

2. The reason for annealing sheet copper is to make it   2.____

   A. soft and easier to work
   B. more resistant to weather
   C. easier to solder
   D. harder and more resistant to blows

3. In draw filing,   3.____

   A. only the edge of the file is used
   B. a triangle file is generally used
   C. the file is pulled toward the mechanic's body in filing
   D. the file must have a safe edge

4. The dimension X on the plate is   4.____
   A. 1 7/8"
   B. 2 1/8"
   C. 2 1/4"
   D. 2 3/8"

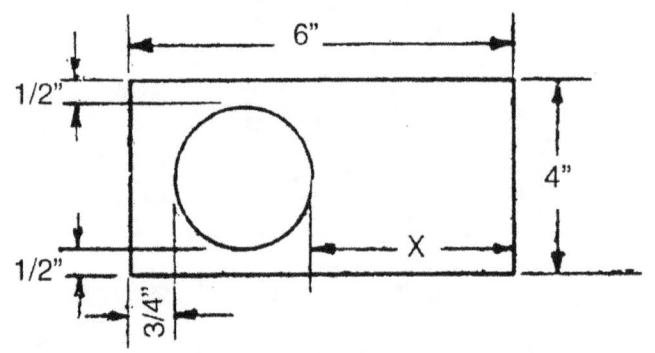

5. One advantage of using a Pittsburgh lock seam when joining two pieces of sheet metal is that, once formed in the shop, it may be assembled anywhere with a   5.____

   A. hickey   B. swage   C. template   D. mallet

6. White cast iron is   6.____

   A. hard and brittle   B. hard and ductile
   C. ductile and malleable   D. brittle and malleable

7. The gage used for measuring copper wire is   7.____

   A. U.S. Standard   B. Stubbs
   C. Washburn and Moen   D. Brown and Sharpe

8. The difference between *right hand* and *left hand* tin snips is the

   A. relative position of the cutting jaws
   B. shape of the cutting jaws
   C. shape of the handles
   D. relative position of the handles

9. A machine used to bend sheet metal is called a

   A. router   B. planer   C. brake   D. swage

10. The type of solder that would be used in *hard soldering* would be _____ solder.

    A. bismuth   B. wiping   C. 50-50   D. silver

11. The MAXIMUM number of 2 inch by 3 inch rectangular pieces which can be cut from the metal sheet is
    A. 8
    B. 6
    C. 4
    D. 2

    METAL SHEET 5 1/4" × 8 1/4"

12. The thin sheet piece when properly folded will form a closed box with a square top and bottom.
    Dimension Z of the box will be
    A. 2
    B. 4
    C. 6
    D. 8

    THIN SHEET PIECE 16"   BOX 10"

13. Sheet metal seams are sometimes grooved. The MAIN function of the grooving is to

    A. facilitate making a soldered joint
    B. prevent unlocking
    C. improve the appearance of the joint
    D. save sheet metal

14. The area, in square inches, of the plate shown at the right is
    A. 32
    B. 52
    C. 58
    D. 64

    5", 8", 4", 8"

15. Shown at the right is an open-top round tin container. In order to make the container so that the metal used for the bottom area (R^2) is equal to the metal used for the cylindrical side area ($2\pi Rh$), the radius R must be equal to
    A. 1/2"
    B. 1"
    C. 2"
    D. 4"

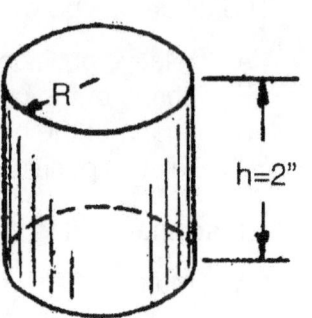

16. On a drawing, the following standard cross-section represents MOST NEARLY
    A. malleable iron
    B. steel
    C. bronze
    D. lead

17. On the curved metal sheet, the distance X is, in inches,
    A. 3
    B. 4
    C. 5
    D. 6

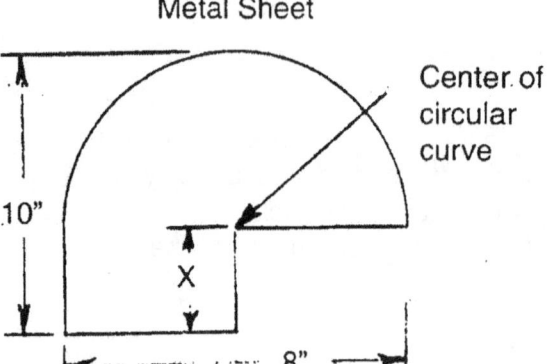

18. If the piece of sheet metal is to be cylindrically formed into a hand scoop by soldering edges X and Y together, then the resultant scoop will be No.
    A. 1
    B. 2
    C. 3
    D. 4

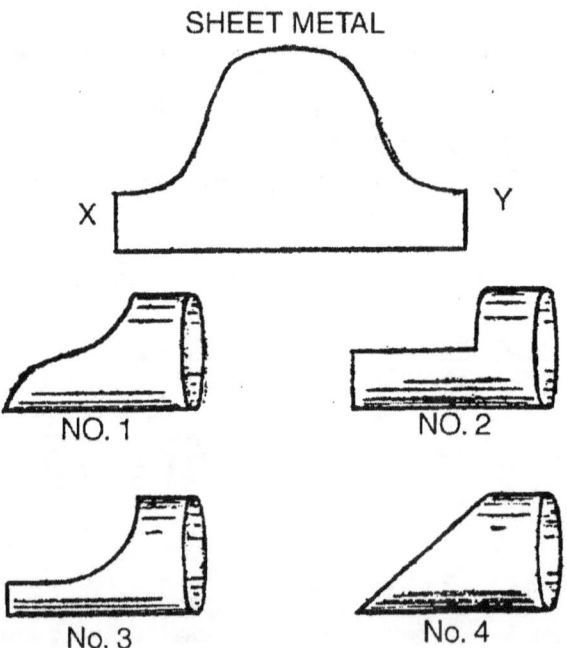

19. Copper sheet is USUALLY specified in

   A. Birmingham gage
   B. ounces per square foot
   C. ounces per square yard
   D. pounds per square yard

   19.____

20. The United States Standard Gage is used to measure sheet metal thicknesses of

   A. tin
   B. aluminum
   C. bronze
   D. iron and steel

   20.____

KEY (CORRECT ANSWERS)

1.	A	11.	B
2.	A	12.	B
3.	C	13.	B
4.	C	14.	C
5.	D	15.	D
6.	A	16.	C
7.	D	17.	D
8.	A	18.	A
9.	C	19.	C
10.	D	20.	D

TOOLS

EXAMINATION SECTION
TEST 1

DIRECTIONS: Each question or incomplete statement is followed by several suggested answers or completions. Select the one that BEST answers the question or completes the statement. *PRINT THE LETTER OF THE CORRECT ANSWER IN THE SPACE AT THE RIGHT.*

1. It is NOT good practice to cut thin-walled copper tubing with an ordinary three-wheel pipe cutter because 1.____

    A. the cutters will be dulled
    B. too much time is required
    C. the tubing end must be reamed after cutting
    D. the tubing is likely to collapse

2. Wedges are used under vertical shoring timbers to 2.____

    A. utilize scrap wood
    B. permit the use of very short timbers
    C. obtain rigid shoring
    D. absorb construction noise

3. The LONGEST nail of the following is a _____-penny nail. 3.____

    A. 12   B. 10   C. 6   D. 4

4. A commonly used priming coat for structural steel is 4.____

    A. enamel   B. varnish   C. red lead   D. lacquer

5. A nail set is a tool used for 5.____

    A. straightening bent nails
    B. cutting nails to specified size
    C. sinking a nail head in wood
    D. measuring nail size

6. The sketch at the right shows a gauge used to 6.____
    A. measure the depth of a hole
    B. determine if a board has been smoothly planed
    C. check the width of a brick
    D. scribe a line on a board parallel to its edge

7. The gauge box shown at the right is used for measuring the dry volume of a concrete mix. If the gauge box is to have a volume of 1 cubic yard, dimension H must be APPROXIMATELY _____ feet.
   A. 2.39
   B. 1.69
   C. 1.45
   D. .63

Questions 8-27.

DIRECTIONS: Questions 8 through 27 refer to the use of tools shown below. Refer to these tools when answering these questions.

3 (#1)

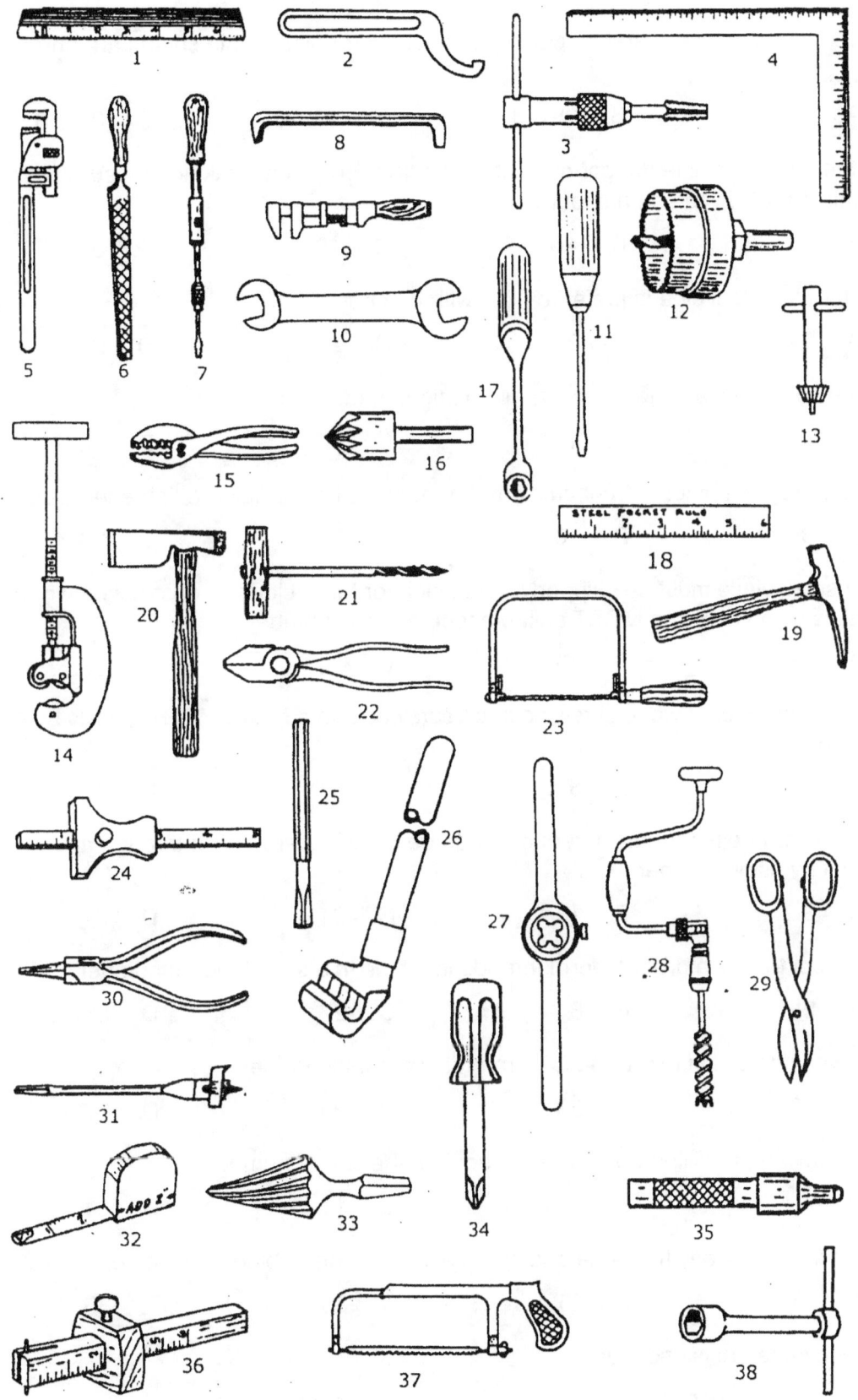

8. Tool number 38 is properly called a(n) _____ wrench. 8.____
   A. box   B. open-end   C. socket   D. tool

9. Two tools which are used for cutting large circular holes in thin sheets are numbers _____ and _____. 9.____
   A. 12; 31   B. 28; 33   C. 12; 28   D. 31; 33

10. If there is a possible danger of electric shock when you are taking measurements, it would be BEST to use number 10.____
    A. 1   B. 4   C. 18   D. 32

11. A 1/2-inch steel pipe is preferably cut with number 11.____
    A. 14   B. 23   C. 27   D. 29

12. A nut for a #8 machine screw should be tightened using number 12.____
    A. 9   B. 15   C. 17   D. 38

13. The hexagon nut for a 1/2-inch diameter machine bolt should be tightened using number 13.____
    A. 5   B. 10   C. 22   D. 26

14. If a small piece must be chipped off a brick in order to clear an obstruction when a brick wall is being built, the MOST suitable tool to use is number 14.____
    A. 16   B. 19   C. 20   D. 33

15. A large number of wood screws can be screwed into a board MOST quickly by using number 15.____
    A. 7   B. 8   C. 11   D. 17

16. A number of different diameter holes can be MOST easily bored through a heavy wood plank by using number 16.____
    A. 3   B. 13   C. 21   D. 31

17. The tool to use in order to form threads in a hole in a steel block is number 17.____
    A. 2   B. 3   C. 27   D. 31

18. Curved designs in thin wood are preferably cut with number 18.____
    A. 12   B. 23   C. 29   D. 37

19. The driving of Phillips-head screws requires the use of number 19.____
    A. 7   B. 8   C. 11   D. 34

20. In order to properly flare one end of a piece of copper tubing, the tool to use is number 20.____
    A. 13   B. 25   C. 33   D. 35

21. Tool number 16 is used for 21.____
    A. counterboring   B. cutting concrete
    C. countersinking   D. reaming

22. A tool that can be used to drill a hole in a concrete wall to install a lead anchor is number
    A. 3 B. 16 C. 21 D. 25

23. After cutting a piece of steel pipe, the burrs are BEST removed from the inside edge with number
    A. 6 B. 13 C. 16 D. 33

24. The MOST convenient tool for measuring the depth of a 1/2-inch diameter hole is number
    A. 24 B. 31 C. 32 D. 36

25. A 1" x 1" x 1/8" angle iron would usually be cut using number
    A. 12 B. 26 C. 29 D. 37

26. Wood screws located in positions NOT accessible to an ordinary screwdriver would be removed using number
    A. 2 B. 8 C. 13 D. 30

27. A small hole can be quickly bored through an 1/8-inch thick plywood board with number
    A. 3 B. 7 C. 21 D. 31

28. The hammer shown to the right would be used by a
    A. carpenter
    B. bricklayer
    C. tinsmith
    D. plumber

29. Which of the following pairs of tools would be used to tighten a nut on a screw?
    A. Two open-end wrenches
    B. One open-end wrench and one adjustable wrench
    C. A screwdriver and a wrench
    D. A vise wrench and an adjustable screwdriver

30. In order to determine if a surface is truly horizontal, it should be checked with a
    A. carpenter's square
    B. plumb bob
    C. steel rule
    D. spirit level

KEY (CORRECT ANSWERS)

1.	D	16.	D
2.	C	17.	B
3.	A	18.	B
4.	C	19.	D
5.	C	20.	D
6.	D	21.	C
7.	B	22.	D
8.	C	23.	D
9.	A	24.	A
10.	A	25.	D
11.	A	26.	B
12.	C	27.	C
13.	B	28.	B
14.	B	29.	C
15.	A	30.	D

TEST 2

DIRECTIONS: Each question or incomplete statement is followed by several suggested answers or completions. Select the one that BEST answers the question or completes the statement. *PRINT THE LETTER OF THE CORRECT ANSWER IN THE SPACE AT THE RIGHT.*

1. After a wedge-shaped hole has been cut into the large stone, the three-legged lifting device is inserted to lift the stone. The CORRECT order for inserting the three legs is
   A. 1, 2, 3
   B. 3, 2, 1
   C. 2, 3, 1
   D. 1, 3, 2

   1.____

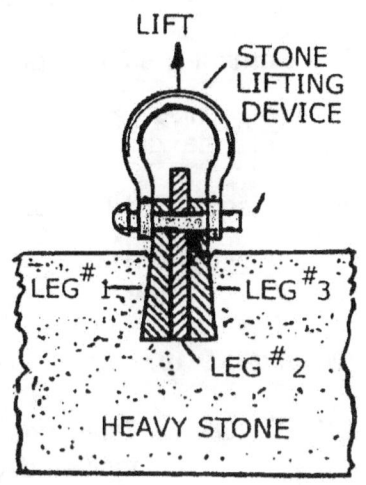

2. Brushes which have been used to apply shellac are BEST cleaned with

   A. alcohol
   B. water
   C. carbon tetrachloride
   D. acetic acid

   2.____

3. When timbers are bolted together, a flat washer is GENERALLY used under the head of the bolt to

   A. prevent the bolt from turning
   B. increase the strength of the bolt
   C. reduce crushing of the wood when the bolt is tightened
   D. make it easier to turn the bolt

   3.____

4. A claw hammer is PROPERLY used for

   A. driving a cold chisel
   B. driving brads
   C. setting rivets
   D. flattening a 1/4" metal bar

   4.____

5. Open-end wrenches are made with the sides of the jaws at about a 15° angle to the line of the handle. This angle

   A. is useful when working the wrench in close quarters
   B. increases the strength of the jaws
   C. prevents extending the handle with a piece of pipe
   D. serves only to improve the appearance of the wrench

   5.____

81

6. It is BEST to cut a piece of sheet metal with a pair of snips by starting each cut with the metal sheet

   A. out near the points of the snips
   B. as far back in the jaws as possible
   C. midway between the snip points and the pivot
   D. one-quarter the way between the snip points and the pivot

7. Cement-lined drain pipe should be cut with a

   A. chisel   B. file
   C. star drill   D. hacksaw

8. A riser is GENERALLY a pipe run which is

   A. horizontal   B. curved
   C. vertical   D. at a 45 angle

Questions 9-18.

DIRECTIONS: Questions 9 through 18 refer to the use of the tools shown below. Read the item, and for the operation given, select the PROPER tool to be used from those shown.

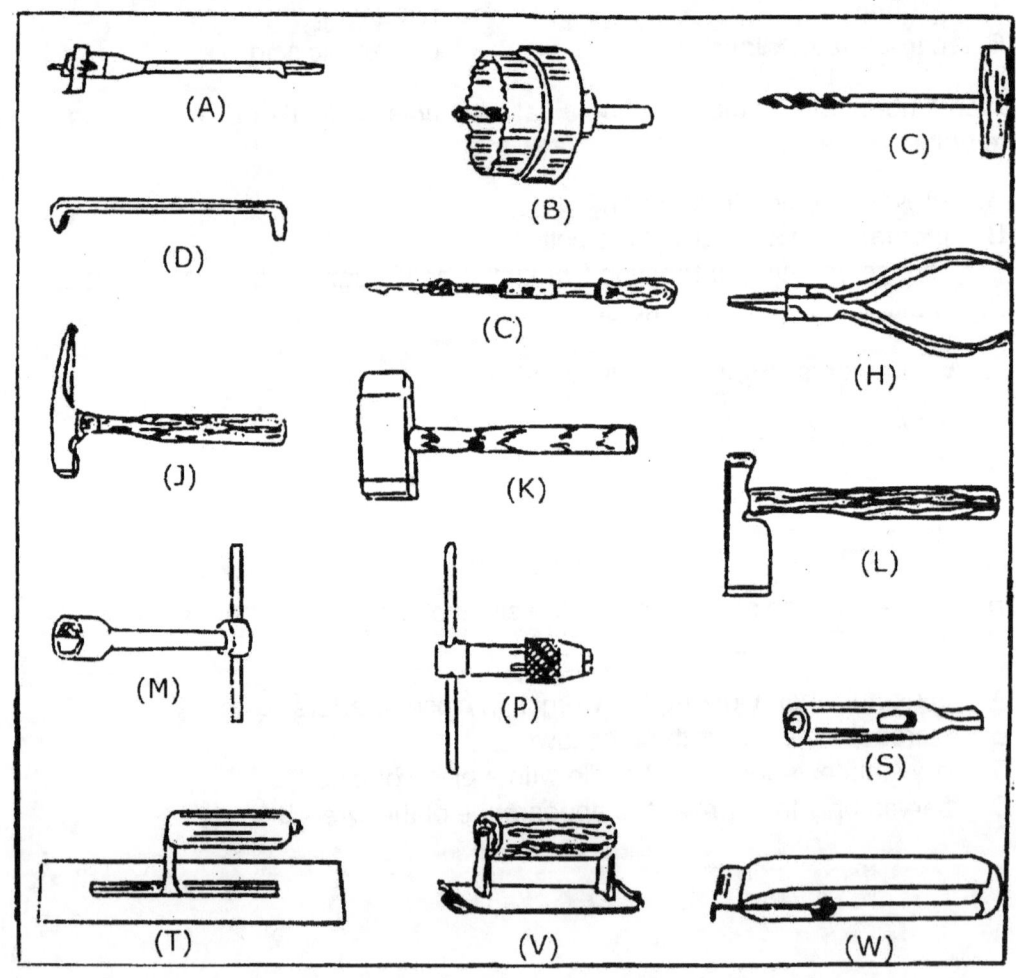

3 (#2)

9. Turning a screw tap when threading a hole in a steel block. 9._____

10. Boring a number of different diameter holes through a heavy wood plank. 10._____

11. Quickly screwing a number of wood screws into a board. 11._____

12. Setting a groove in a cement floor before hardening of the cement. 12._____

13. Plastering a wall. 13._____

14. Chipping a small piece out of a brick to clear a projecting steel rod when building a brick wall. 14._____

15. Tightening a large nut. 15._____

16. Quickly boring a small hole through a 1/8" board. 16._____

17. Unfastening wood screws located in a position inaccessible to an ordinary screwdriver. 17._____

18. Making a 1 1/2" hole in a steel plate. 18._____

19. A pneumatic bucker is used in 19._____

    A. riveting   B. brazing
    C. soldering   D. reinforcing concrete

20. To make certain two points separated by a vertical distance of 8 feet are in perfect vertical alignment, it would be BEST to use a 20._____

    A. surface gage   B. height gage
    C. protractor   D. plumb bob

21. When repair work is being done on the elevated structure, canvas spreads are suspended under the working area MAINLY to 21._____

    A. reduce noise   B. discourage crowds
    C. protect the structure   D. protect pedestrians

22. When grinding a weld smooth, it is MOST important to avoid 22._____

    A. overheating the surrounding metal
    B. grinding too much of the weld away
    C. grinding too slowly
    D. grinding after the weld has cooled off

23. A gouge is a tool used for 23._____

    A. planing wood smooth   B. grinding metal
    C. drilling steel   D. chiseling wood

24. The tool that should be used to cut a 1" x 4" plank down to a 3" width is a 24._____

    A. hacksaw   B. crosscut saw
    C. rip saw   D. backsaw

25. Threads are cut on the ends of a length of steel pipe by the use of a

    A. brace and bit
    B. counterbore
    C. stock and die
    D. doweling jig

26. A bit brace can be locked so that the bit will turn in only one direction by means of a

    A. feed screw
    B. rachet device
    C. universal chuck
    D. ball-bearing device

27. A reamer is used to

    A. enlarge drilled holes to an exact size
    B. punch holes to desired size
    C. line up adjacent holes
    D. lay out holes before drilling

28. The tool shown at the right is a
    A. countersink
    B. counterbore
    C. star drill
    D. burring reamer

29. The saw shown at the right would be used to cut
    A. curved designs in thin wood
    B. strap iron
    C. asphalt tiles to fit against walls
    D. soft lead pipe

30. The tool shown at the right is a
    A. float
    B. finishing trowel
    C. hawk
    D. roofing seamer

KEY (CORRECT ANSWERS)

1. D
2. A
3. C
4. B
5. A

6. B
7. D
8. C
9. P
10. A

11. E
12. V
13. T
14. J
15. M

16. C
17. D
18. B
19. B
20. D

21. C
22. B
23. D
24. C
25. C

26. B
27. A
28. D
29. A
30. A

TEST 3

DIRECTIONS: Each question or incomplete statement is followed by several suggested answers or completions. Select the one that BEST answers the question or completes the Statement. *PRINT THE LETTER OF THE CORRECT ANSWER IN THE SPACE AT THE RIGHT.*

Questions 1-8.

DIRECTIONS: Questions 1 through 8 are to be answered on the basis of the following items. The sizes of the items shown are NOT their actual sizes. Each item is identified by a number, For each question, select the answer which gives the identifying number of the item that BEST answers the question.

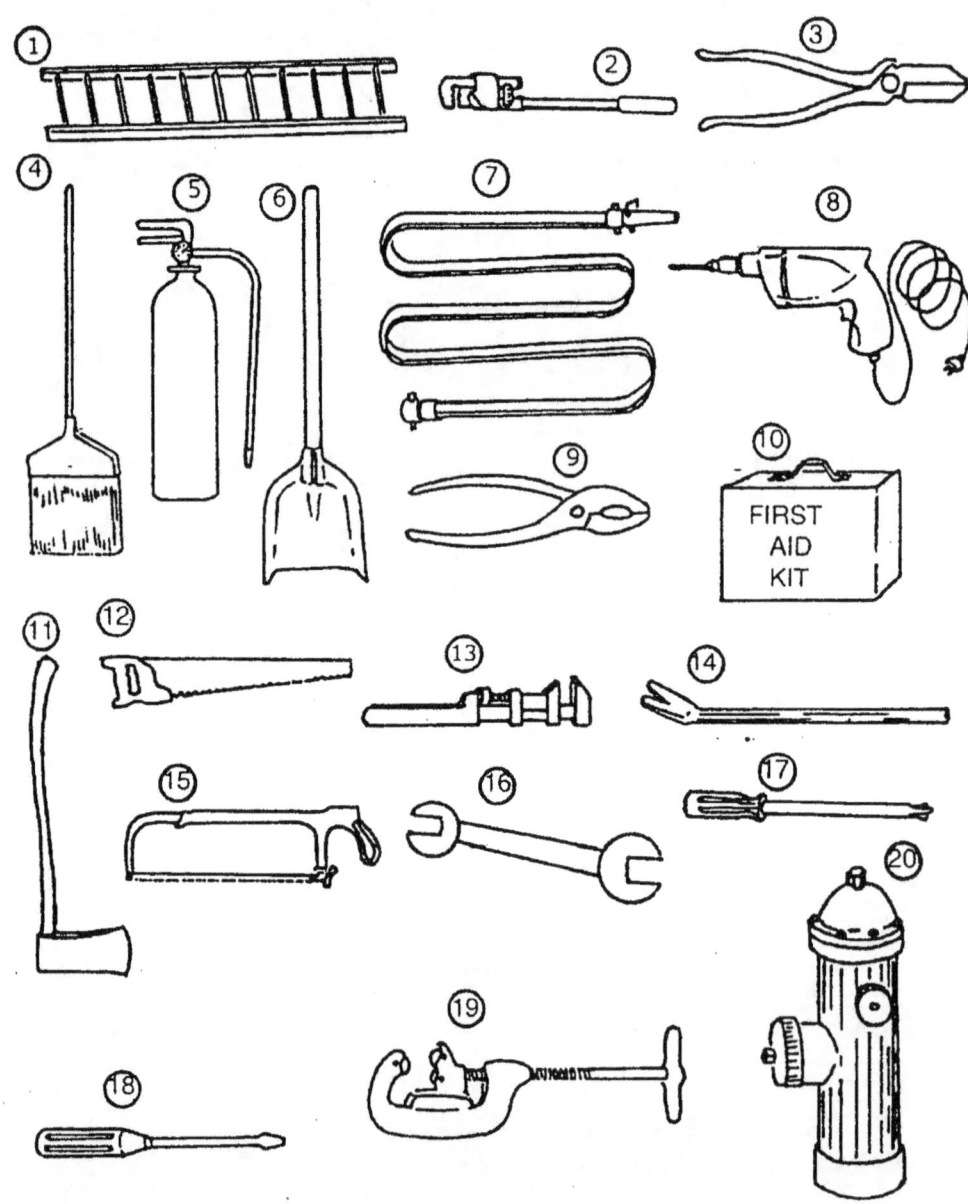

1. Which one of the following items should be connected to a hydrant and used to put out a fire?
   A. 5   B. 7   C. 8   D. 17

2. Which one of the following pairs of items should be used after a fire to clean a floor covered with small pieces of burned material?
   A. 1 and 14   B. 4 and 6   C. 10 and 12   D. 11 and 13

3. Which one of the following pairs of items should be used for cutting a branch from a tree?
   A. 2 and 3   B. 8 and 9   C. 11 and 12   D. 14 and 15

4. Which one of the following items should be used to rescue a victim from a second floor window?
   A. 1   B. 10   C. 15   D. 20

5. Which one of the following pairs of items should be used to tighten a nut on a screw?
   A. 2 and 3   B. 8 and 19   C. 9 and 14   D. 16 and 18

6. Which one of the following items should be used to repair a leaky faucet?
   A. 4   B. 5   C. 12   D. 13

7. Which one of the following items should be used as a source of water at a fire?
   A. 2   B. 6   C. 9   D. 20

8. Which item should be used for cutting metal?
   A. 6   B. 13   C. 15   D. 18

Questions 9-18.

DIRECTIONS: Questions 9 through 18, inclusive, in Column I are articles or terms used in structure maintenance and repair work, each of which is associated primarily (though not exclusively) with one of the trade specialties listed in Column II. For each article or term in Column I, select the trade specialty from Column II in which it is in greatest use. Indicate in the space at the right, the letter preceding your selected trade specialty.

COLUMN I
(Articles or Terms)

9. Drift pin
10. Studding
11. Elbow
12. Header course
13. Dowel
14. Screeding
15. Cleanout
16. Air jam
17. Curing
18. Mortise and tenon

COLUMN II
(Trade Specialties)

A. Carpentry
B. Masonry
C. Ironwork
D. Plumbing

19. Practically all valves used in plumbing work are made so that the handwheel is turned clockwise instead of counterclockwise to close the valve.
    The PROBABLE reason is that

    A. it is easier to remember since screws and nuts move inward when turned clockwise
    B. the handwheel is less likely to loosen
    C. greater force can be exerted
    D. most people are righthanded

20. Sharpening a hand saw consists of

    A. jointing, shaping, setting, and filing
    B. adzing, clinching, forging, and machining
    C. brazing, chiseling, grinding, and mitering
    D. bushing, dressing, lapping, and machining

21. A hacksaw blade having 32 teeth to the inch is the BEST blade to use when cutting

    A. cold rolled steel shafting
    B. wrought iron pipe
    C. stainless steel plate
    D. copper tubing

22. Good practice dictates that an adjustable open-end wrench should be used PRIMARILY when the

    A. nut to be turned is soft and must not be scored
    B. extra leverage is needed
    C. proper size of fixed wrench is not available
    D. location is cramped permitting only a small turning angle

23. When a hacksaw blade is designated as an 18-32, the numbers 18 and 32 refer to, respectively, the blade's

    A. stroke and thickness
    B. thickness and length
    C. length and teeth per inch
    D. teeth per inch and stroke

24. When a machine screw is designated as a 10-32, the numbers 10 and 32 refer to, respectively, the screw's

    A. length and head type
    B. threads per inch and length
    C. diameter and threads per inch
    D. head type and diameter

25. An offset screwdriver is MOST useful for turning a wood screw when

    A. a strong force needs to be applied
    B. the screw head is marred
    C. space is limited
    D. speed is desired

26. Of the following orders for tools or materials used in the building trades, the one which is INCOMPLETE is

   A. 1 paintbrush, flat, 2 in. wide
   B. 1 drill, twist, straight shank, high speed, 3/8 in.
   C. 1 snake, steel, 3/4 in. wide by 1/8 in. thick
   D. 1 keg of nails, 10 penny, common wire, galvanized

27. The tool that is GENERALLY used to slightly elongate a round hole in strap-iron is a

   A. rat-tail file   B. reamer
   C. drill   D. rasp

28. The BEST way to locate a point on the floor directly below a given point on the ceiling is by using a

   A. plumber's snake   B. plumb bob
   C. flashlight   D. chalk line

29. The wrench that would prove LEAST useful in uncoupling several pieces of pipe is a _____ wrench.

   A. socket   B. chain   C. strap   D. stillson

30. Of the following, the tool that is LEAST easily broken is a

   A. file   B. pry bar
   C. folding rule   D. hacksaw blade

KEY (CORRECT ANSWERS)

1.	B		16.	C
2.	B		17.	B
3.	C		18.	A
4.	A		19.	A
5.	D		20.	A
6.	D		21.	D
7.	D		22.	C
8.	C		23.	C
9.	C		24.	C
10.	A		25.	C
11.	B		26.	C
12.	D		27.	A
13.	A		28.	B
14.	B		29.	A
15.	D		30.	B

READING COMPREHENSION
UNDERSTANDING AND INTERPRETING WRITTEN MATERIAL

EXAMINATION SECTION

TEST 1

DIRECTIONS: Each question or incomplete statement is followed by several suggested answers or completions. Select the one that BEST answers the question or completes the statement. *PRINT THE LETTER OF THE CORRECT ANSWER IN THE SPACE AT THE RIGHT.*

Questions 1-2.

DIRECTIONS: Questions 1 and 2 are to be answered in accordance with the following paragraph.

Steam cleaners get their name from the fact that steam is used to generate pressure and is also a by-product of heating the cleaning solution. Steam itself has little cleaning power. It will melt some soils, but it does no dissolve them, break them up, or destroy their clinging power. Rather surprisingly, good machines generate as little steam as possible. Modern surface chemistry depends on a chemical solution to dissolve dirt, destroy its clinging power, and hold it in suspension. Steam actually hinders such a solution, but heat helps its physical and chemical action. Cleaning is most efficient when a hot solution reaches the work in heavy volume.

1. In accordance with the above paragraph, for MOST efficient cleaning, 1.____
   A. a heavy volume of steam is needed
   B. hot steam is needed to break up the soils
   C. steam is used to dissolve the surface dirt
   D. a hot chemical solution should always be used

2. With reference to the above paragraph, the steam in a steam cleaner is used to 2.____
   A. generate pressure
   B. create b-product chemicals
   C. slow down the chemical action of the cleaning solution
   D. dissolve accumulations of dirt

Questions 3-5.

DIRECTIONS: Questions 3 through 5 are based on the information given in the following paragraphs. Use ONLY the information given in these paragraphs in answering these questions.

METHOD A: Move voltmeter lead from BAT to GEN terminal of regulator. Retard generator speed until generator voltage is reduced to 2 volts on a 6-volt system or 4 volts on a 12-volt system. Move voltmeter lead back to BAT terminal of regulator. Bring generator back to specified speed and note voltage setting.

METHOD B: Connect a variable resistance into the field circuit. Turn out all resistance. Operate generator at specified speed. Slowly increase (turn in) resistance until generator voltage is reduced to 2 volts on a 6-volt system or 4 volts on a 12-volt system. Turn out all resistance again, and note voltage setting. Regulator cover must be in place. To adjust voltage setting, turn adjusting screw. Turn clockwise to increase setting and counterclockwise to decrease voltage setting.

3. According to the instructions given in the paragraphs, when taking readings,
   A. a variable resistance is to be connected into the generator armature circuit
   B. the generator voltage on a 12-volt system is reduced to 2 volts
   C. the cover is to be in place
   D. the voltmeter lead should be continuously connected to the BAT terminal

4. In following the instructions given in the paragraphs, the one of the following statements that is MOST NEARLY correct is:
   A. The adjusting screw must be turned clockwise to increase the voltage setting
   B. Method B makes use of a fixed resistor
   C. Method A makes use of a variable resistor
   D. The generator voltage is reduced by decreasing the resistance

5. The above instructions pertain MOST likely to a(n)
   A. voltage regulator	B. starting regulator
   C. amperage regulator	D. circuit breaker

Questions 6-7.

DIRECTIONS: Questions 6 and 7 are based upon the following paragraph. Use ONLY the information contained in this paragraph in answering these questions.

With the engine running at normal idling speed and the engine hood open, attach the vacuum gauge to the intake manifold. The vacuum gauge should read about 18 to 21 inches, and the pointer should be steady. A needle fluctuating between 10 and 15 inches may indicate a defective cylinder-head, gasket, or valve. An extremely low reading indicates a leak in the intake manifold or gaskets. Accelerate the engine with full throttle momentarily. Notice if the gauge indicator fails to drop to approximately 2 inches as the throttle is opened, and recoil to at least 24 inches as the throttle is closed. If so, this may be an indication of diluted oil, poor piston-ring sealing, or an abnormal restriction in the exhaust, carburetor, or air cleaner. The above reading apply to sea level. There will be approximately a 1inch drop for each 1,000 feet of altitude.

6. If a vacuum test is made on a properly operating engine at an altitude of 3,000 feet, the vacuum gauge should read MOST NEARLY
   A. 12"	B. 15"	C. 13"	D. 24"

7. If a vacuum test is made on an engine which has an abnormal restriction in the exhaust, this will be evidenced by   7.____
    A. a leak in the intake manifold
    B. the gauge indicator failing to drop to approximately 3 inches on opening the throttle
    C. the gauge fluctuating around 12 inches
    D. a steady high gauge reading

Questions 8-10.

DIRECTIONS: Questions 8 through 10 are to be answered in accordance with the information in the following paragraph.

The following is a set of instructions on engine shut-down procedure: When an engine equipped with an electric shut-down valve is used, the engine can be shut down completely by turning off the switch key on installations equipped with an electric shut-down valve, or by turning the manual shut-down valve lever. Turning off the switch key which controls the electric shut-down valve always stops the engine unless the override button on the shutdown valve has been locked in the open position. If the manual override on the electric shut-down valve is being used, turn the button full counterclockwise to stop the engine.
CAUTION: Never leave the switch key or the override button in the valve open or run position when the engine is not running. With overhead tanks, this would allow fuel to drain into the cylinder, causing hydraulic lock.

8. According to the above paragraph, it becomes apparent that if an engine does not stop when the electric shut-down valve switch key is shut off,   8.____
    A. an open manual switch is present
    B. the override button is locked in the closed position
    C. a closed manual switch is functioning
    D. the override button is locked in the open position

9. When using an engine equipped with an electric shut-down valve,   9.____
    A. no alternate method is available
    B. a manual method is not present
    C. a manual override can shut the engine down
    D. a manual override will not work

10. As a matter of caution, the switch key in the closed position or the override button in the stop position will   10.____
    A. assist in keeping fuel in the cylinders
    B. prevent fuel from flooding the cylinder cavities
    C. assist in producing hydraulic lock
    D. aid fuel dilution

Questions 11-12.

DIRECTIONS: Questions 11 and 12 are to be answered according to the information given in the following paragraph.

You have been instructed to expedite the fabrication of four special salt spreader trucks using chassis that are available in the shop. All four trucks must be delivered before the opening of business on December 1. Based on workload and available hours, the foreman of the body shop indicates that he could manufacture one complete salt spreader body in five weeks, with one additional week required for mounting and securing each body to the available chassis. No work could begin on the body until the engines and hydraulic component, which would have to be purchased, were available for use. The Purchasing Department has promised delivery of engines and hydraulic components three months after the order is placed. (Assume that all months have four weeks, and the same crew is doing the assembling and manufacturing.)

11. With reference to the above paragraph, assuming that the Purchasing Department placed the order at the beginning of the first week in February and ultimate delivery of the engines and components was delayed by six weeks, the date of completion of the first salt spreader truck would be CLOSEST to the end of the _____ week in _____. 11.____
  A. fourth; July
  B. second; August
  C. fourth; August
  D. first; September

12. With reference to the above paragraph, the LATEST date that the engines and associated hydraulic components could be requisitioned in order to meet the specified deadline would be CLOSEST to the beginning of the _____ week in _____. 12.____
  A. first; February
  B. first; March
  C. third; March
  D. first; April

Questions 13-20.

DIRECTIONS: Questions 13 through 20 are based on the paragraph on JACKS shown below. When answering these questions, refer to this paragraph.

JACKS

When using a jack, a workman should check the capacity plate or other markings on the jack to make sure the device is heavy enough to support the load. Where there is no plate, capacity should be determined and painted on the side of the jack. The workman should see that jacks are well lubricated, but only at points where lubrication is specified, and should inspect them for broken teeth or faulty holding fixtures. A jack should never be thrown or dropped upon the floor; such treatment may crack or distort the metal, thus causing the jack to break when a load is lifted. It is important that the floor or ground surface upon which the jack is placed be level and clean, and the safe limit of floor loading is not exceeded. If the surface is earth, the jack base should be set on heavy wood blocking, preferably hardwood, of sufficient size that the blocking will not turn over, shift, or sink. If the surface is not perfectly level, the jack may be set on blocking, which should be leveled by wedges securely placed so that they cannot be brushed or forced out of place. Extenders of wood or metal, intended to provide a higher rise where a jack cannot reach up to load or lift it high enough, should never be used. Instead, a larger jack should be obtained or higher blocking which is correspondingly wider and longer should be placed under the jack. All lifts should be vertical with the jack correctly centered for the lift. The base of the jack should be on a perfectly level surface, and the jack head, with its hardwood shim, should bear against a perfectly level meeting surface.

13. To make sure the jack is heavy enough to support a certain load, the workman should
    A. lubricate the jack
    B. shim the jack
    C. check the capacity plate
    D. use a long handle

14. A jack should be lubricated
    A. after using
    B. before painting
    C. only at specified points
    D. to prevent slipping

15. The workman should inspect a jack for
    A. manufacturer's name
    B. broken teeth
    C. paint peeling
    D. broken wedges

16. Metal parts on a jack may crack if
    A. the jack is thrown on the floor
    B. the load is leveled
    C. blocking is used
    D. the handle is too short

17. It would not be a safe practice for a workman to
    A. center the jack under the load
    B. set the jack on a level surface
    C. use hardwood for blocking
    D. use extenders to reach up to the load

18. Wedges may safely be used to
    A. replace a broken tooth
    B. prevent the overloading of a jack
    C. level the blocking under a jack
    D. straighten distorted metal

19. Blocking should be
    A. made of a soft wood
    B. placed between the jack base and the earth surface
    C. well lubricated
    D. used to repair a broken tooth

20. A hardwood shim should be used
    A. between the head and its meeting surface
    B. under the jack
    C. as a filler
    D. to level a surface

Questions 21-22.

DIRECTIONS: Questions 21 and 22 are to be answered ONLY on the basis of the information contained in the following paragraph.

Many experiments have been made on the effects of alcoholic beverages. These studies show that alcohol decreases alertness and efficiency. It decreases self-consciousness and, at the same time, increases confidence and feelings of ease and relaxation. It impairs attention and judgment. It destroys fear of consequences. Usual cautions are thrown to the winds. Habit systems become disorganized. The driver who uses alcohol tends to disregard his usual safety practices. He may not even be aware that he is disregarding them. His reaction time slows down; normally quick reactions are not possible for him. To make matters worse, he may not realize he is slower. His eye muscles may be so affected that his vision is not normal. He cannot correctly judge the speed of his car or of any other car. He cannot correctly estimate distances being covered by each. He becomes a highway menace.

21. The paragraph states that the drinking of alcohol makes a driver 21.____
   A. *more* alert
   B. *less* confident
   C. *more* efficient
   D. *less* attentive

22. From the above paragraph, it is reasonable to assume that a driver may overcome the bad effects of drinking alcohol by 22.____
   A. being more cautious
   B. relying on his good driving habits to a greater extent than normally
   C. watching the road more carefully
   D. waiting for the alcohol to wear off before drinking

Questions 23-25.

DIRECTIONS: Each question consists of a statement. You are to indicate whether the statement is TRUE (T) or FALSE (F). PRINT THE LETTER OF THE CORRECT ANSWER IN THE SPACE AT THE RIGHT.

When in use, the storage battery becomes hot, and water evaporate from the cells of the battery, so clean water preferably distilled, must be added at frequent intervals. This action keeps the level of the battery liquid above the top of the battery plates.

23. All water loss from a storage battery occurs when the battery is in use. 23.____

24. The water added to a storage battery does not have to be distilled. 24.____

25. Water in the storage battery must be kept level with the top of the battery plates. 25.____

KEY (CORRECT ANSWERS)

1.	D		11.	A
2.	A		12.	B
3.	C		13.	C
4.	A		14.	C
5.	A		15.	B
6.	B		16.	A
7.	B		17.	D
8.	D		18.	C
9.	C		19.	B
10.	B		20.	A

21. D
22. F
23. F
24. T
25. F

TEST 2

DIRECTIONS: Each question or incomplete statement is followed by several suggested answers or completions. Select the one that BEST answers the question or completes the statement. *PRINT THE LETTER OF THE CORRECT ANSWER IN THE SPACE AT THE RIGHT.*

Questions 1-2.

DIRECTIONS: Questions 1 and 2 are based on the following paragraph

Because electric drills run at high speed, the cutting edges of a twist drill are heated quickly. If the metal is thick, the drill point must be withdrawn from the hole frequently to cool it and clear out chips. Forcing the drill continuously into a deep hole will heat it, thereby spoiling its temper and cutting edges. A portable electric drill has the advantage that it can be taken to the work and used to drill holes in material too large to handle in a drill press.

1. According to the above paragraph, overheating of a twist drill will 1.____
   A. slow down the work
   B. cause excessive drill breakage
   C. dull the drill
   D. spoil the accuracy of the work

2. According to the above paragraph, one method of preventing overheating of 2.____
   a twist drill is to
   A. use cooling oil
   B. drill a smaller pilot hole first
   C. use a drill press
   D. remove the drill from the work frequently

Questions 3-5.

DIRECTIONS: Questions 3 through 5, inclusive, are to be answered in accordance with the paragraph below.

A steam heating system with steam having a pressure of less than 10 pounds is called a low-pressure system. The majority of steam-heating systems are of this type. The steam may be provided by low-pressure boilers installed *expressly* for the purpose, or it may be generated in boiler at a higher pressure and reduced in pressure before admitted to the heating mains. In other instances, it may be possible to use exhaust steam which has been made to run engines and other machines and which still contains enough heat to be utilized in the heating system. The first case represents the system of heating used in the ordinary residence or other small building; the other two represent the systems of heating employed in industrial buildings where a power plant is installed for general power purposes.

3. According to the above paragraph, whether or not a steam heating system is 3.____
   considered a low pressure system is determined by the pressure
   A. generated by the boiler
   B. in the heating main
   C. at the inlet side of the reducing valve
   D. of the exhaust

4. According to the above paragraph, steam used for heating is sometimes obtained from steam
   A. generated principally to operate machinery
   B. exhausted from larger boilers
   C. generated at low pressure and brought up to high pressure before being used
   D. generated by engines other than boilers

5. As used in the above paragraph, the word *expressly* means
   A. rapidly   B. specifically   C. usually   D. mainly

Questions 6-7.

DIRECTIONS: Questions 6 and 7 are to be answered in accordance with the following paragraph.

When one is making the selection of grinding wheel specifications, the first variable factor to consider is the wheel speed, which influences the grade and the bond of the wheel. It is recommended that the grade should be determined in this way: the higher the wheel speed with relation to work speed, the softer the wheel should be. When, for any reason, the wheel speed is reduced, then it may be expected that the wheel will wear faster, but this can be overcome by choosing a wheel of a harder grade, assuming that the grade was correct for the initial speed.

6. It can be said that the MOST important piece of information in the above paragraph is:
   A. The higher the relative wheel speed, the softer should be the wheel
   B. Wheel speed is a variable factor
   C. At low speeds wheels wear rapidly
   D. When a wheel slows down, it should be replaced by a harder grade

7. According to the above paragraph, no indication is made that
   A. there are other factor too be considered beside speed
   B. hard wheels at low speed wear faster than soft wheels at high speed
   C. the lower the speed, the harder should be the grade
   D. the selection of the bond of the wheel is affected by speed

Questions 8-9.

DIRECTIONS: Questions 8 and 9 are to be answered ONLY according to the information in the following paragraph.

Metal spraying is used for many purposes. Worn bearings on shafts and spindles can be readily restored to original dimensions with any desired metal or alloy. Low-carbon steel shafts may be supplied with high-carbon steel journal surfaces, which can then be ground to size after spraying. By using babbitt wire, bearings can be lined or babbitted while rotating. Pump shafts and impellers can be coated with any desired metal to overcome wear and corrosion. Valve seats may be re-surfaced. Defective castings can be repaired by filling in blow-holes and checks. The application of metal spraying to the field of corrosion resistance is growing, although the major application in this field is in the use of sprayed zinc. Tin, lead, and aluminum have been used considerably. The process is used for structural and tank applications in the field as well as in the shop.

8. According to the above paragraph, worn bearing surfaces on shafts are metal-sprayed in order to
   A. prevent corrosion of the shaft
   B. fit them into larger-sized impellers
   C. return them to their original sizes
   D. replace worn babbitt metal

8.____

9. According to the above paragraph, rotating bearings can be metal-sprayed using
   A. babbitt wire
   B. high-carbon steel
   C. low-carbon steel
   D. any desired metal

9.____

Questions 10-11.

DIRECTIONS: Questions 10 and 11 are to be answered ONLY according to the information in the following paragraph.

The wheels used for internal grinding should general be softer than those used for other grinding operations because the contact area between the wheel and work is comparatively large. A soft wheel that will cut with little pressure should be used to prevent springing the spindle. The grade of the wheel depends upon the character of the work and the stiffness of the machine; and where a large variety of work is being ground, it may not be practicable to have an assortment of wheels adapted to all conditions. By adjusting the speed, however, a wheel not exactly suited to the work in hand can often be used. If the wheel wears too rapidly, it should be run faster; and if it tends to glaze, the speed should be diminished.

10. On the basis of the above passage only, it may BEST be said that
    A. the type and grade of wheel are independent of the sturdiness of the machine
    B. by increasing the wheel speed, parts can easily be internally ground
    C. wheels used for outside grinding usually have a smaller contact area between the wheel and work
    D. to carry on hand an assortment of wheels for all conceivable internal grinding jobs is economical

10.____

11. On the basis of the above passage only, it may BEST be said that
    A. in general, if a wheel wears too rapidly, the speed should be decreased
    B. by decreasing the wheel speed, a wheel not quite appropriate for the job may sometimes be used
    C. where a large variety of work is being ground, the grade of wheel depends on the diameter of the wheel
    D. if a wheel tends to glaze, it should run faster

11.____

Questions 12-15.

DIRECTIONS: Questions 12 through 15, inclusive, are to be answered ONLY in accordance with the following paragraph.

Cylindrical surfaces are the most common form of finished surface found on machine parts, although flat surfaces are also very common; hence, many metal-cutting *processes* are for the purpose of producing either cylindrical or flat surfaces. The machines used for cylindrical or flat shapes may be, and often are, utilized also for forming the various irregular or special shapes required on many machine parts. Because of the prevalence of cylindrical and flat surfaces, the student of manufacturing practice should learn first about the machines and methods employed to produce these surfaces. The cylindrical surfaces may be internal as in holes and cylinders. Any one part may, of course, have cylindrical sections of different diameters and lengths and include flat end or shoulders; and frequently there is a threaded part or possibly some finished surface that is not circular in cross-section. The prevalence of cylindrical surfaces on machine parts explains why lathes are found in all machine shops. It is important to understand the various uses of the lathe because many of the operations are the same fundamentally as those performed on other types of machine tools.

12. According to the above paragraph, the MOST common form of finished surfaces found on machine parts is
    A. cylindrical   B. elliptical   C. flat   D. square

13. According to the above paragraph, any one part of cylindrical surface may have
    A. chases   B. shoulders   C. keyways   D. splines

14. According to the above paragraph, lathes are found in all machine shops because cylindrical surfaces on machine parts are
    A. scarce   B. internal   C. common   D. external

15. As used in the above paragraph, the work *processes* means
    A. operations   B. purposes   C. devices   D. tools

Questions 16-17.

DIRECTIONS: Questions 16 and 17 are to be answered ONLY in accordance with the following paragraph.

The principle of interchangeability requires manufacture to such specification that component parts of a device may be selected at random and assembled to fit and operate satisfactorily. Interchangeable manufacture, therefore, requires that parts be made to definite limits of error and to fit gages instead of mating parts. Interchangeability does not necessarily involve a high degree of precision; stove lids, for example, are interchangeable but are not particularly accurate, and carriage bolts and nuts are not precision products but are completely interchangeable. Interchangeability may be employed in unit production as well as mass production systems of manufacture.

16. According to the above paragraph, in order for parts to be interchangeable, they must be
    A. precision-machined
    B. selectively-assembled
    C. mass-produced
    D. made to fit gages

17. According to the above paragraph, carriage bolts are interchangeable because they are
    A. precision-made
    B. sized to specific tolerances
    C. individually matched products
    D. produced in small units

Questions 18-22.

DIRECTIONS: Questions 18 through 22 are to be answered in accordance with the following passage.

TITANIC AIR COMPRESSOR

Valves: The compressors are equipped with Titanic plate valves which are automatic in operation. Valves are so constructed that an entire valve assembly can readily be removed from the head. The valves provide large port area with short lift and are accurately guided to insure positive seating.

Starting Unloader: Each compressor (or air end) is equipped with a centrifugal governor which is bolted directly to the compressor crankshaft. The governor actuates cylinder relief valves so as to relieve pressure from the cylinders during starting and stopping. The motor is never required to start the compressor under load.

Air Strainer: Each cylinder air inlet connection is fitted with a suitable combination air strainer and muffler.

Pistons: Pistons are lightweight castings, ribbed internally to secure strength, and are accurately turned and ground. Each piston is fitted with four (4) rings, two of which are oil control rings. Piston pins are hardened and tempered steel of the full floating type. Bronze bushings are used between piston pin and piston.

Connecting Rods: Connecting rods are of solid bronze designed for maximum strength, rigidity, and wear. Crank pins are fitted with renewable steel bushings. Connecting rods are of the one-piece type, there being no bolts, nuts, or cotter pins which can come loose. With this type of construction, wear is reduced to a negligible amount, and adjustment of wrist pin and crank pin bearings is unnecessary.

Main Bearings: Main bearings are of the ball type and are securely held in position by spacers. This type of bearing entirely eliminates the necessity of frequent adjustment or attention. The crankshaft is always in perfect alignment.

Crankshaft: The crankshaft is a one-piece heat-treated forging of best quality open-hearth steel, of rugged design, and of sufficient size to transmit the motor power and any additional stresses which may occur in service. Each crankshaft is counter-balanced (dynamically balanced) to reduce vibration to a minimum, and is accurately machined to properly receive the ball bearing races, crank pin bushing, flexible coupling, and centrifugal governor. Suitable provision is made to insure proper lubrication of all crankshaft bearings and bushings with the minimum amount of attention.

Coupling: Compressor and motor shafts are connected through a Morse Chain Company all-metal enclosed flexible coupling. This coupling consists of two sprockets, one mounted on, and keyed to, each shaft; the sprockets are wrapped by a single Morse Chain, the entire assembly being enclosed in a split aluminum grease packed cover.

18. The crank pin of the connecting rod is fitted with a renewable bushing made of 18.____
    A. solid bronze B. steel
    C. slight-weight casting D. ball bearings

19. When the connecting rod is of the one-piece type, 19.____
    A. the wrist pins require frequent adjustment
    B. the crank pins require frequent adjustment
    C. the cotter pins frequently will come loose
    D. wear is reduced to a negligible amount

20. The centrifugal governor is bolted DIRECTLY to the 20.____
    A. compressor crankshaft B. main bearing
    C. piston pin D. muffler

21. The number of oil control rings required for each piston is 21.____
    A. one B. two C. three D. four

22. The compressor and motor shafts are connected through a flexible coupling. 22.____
    These couplings are _____ to the shafts.
    A. keyed B. brazed C. soldered D. press fit

Questions 23-25.

DIRECTIONS: Questions 23 through 25, inclusive, are to be answered in accordance with the following paragraph.

Wherever a soil pipe has to be provided for in a partition, special care must be taken that the hubs do not project beyond the finish face of the plaster. Before framing a building, it is desirable to ascertain where the stacks are and to provide for them. Building regulations require the stacks to be of 4-inch cast-iron even in small dwellings. With a 4-inch stack, the hub is 6 1/8 inches in diameter; and, therefore, 2 by 6 studs must be used. Special care should be taken that no plaster comes in contact with a soil pipe for *subsequent* settlement may cause cracking.

23. As used in the above paragraph, *subsequent* means MOST NEARLY 23.____
    A. heavy B. sudden C. later D. soon

24. According to the above paragraph, 4" cast-iron soil pipes are used because
    A. they will not project beyond the face of the plaster
    B. it is easier to plaster over 4" pipe
    C. they can be located easier
    D. they are required by law

25. According to the above paragraph, the reason plaster should NOT be in direct contact with soil pipe is because
    A. the plaster would be damaged by moisture
    B. rust will bleed through the plaster
    C. of the possibility of cracks due to settlement
    D. it is harder to plaster over 4" pipe

KEY (CORRECT ANSWERS)

1.	C	11.	B
2.	D	12.	A
3.	B	13.	B
4.	A	14.	C
5.	B	15.	A
6.	A	16.	D
7.	B	17.	B
8.	C	18.	B
9.	A	19.	D
10.	C	20.	A

21.	B
22.	A
23.	C
24.	D
25.	C

ARITHMETICAL REASONING
EXAMINATION SECTION
TEST 1

DIRECTIONS: Each question or incomplete statement is followed by several suggested answers or completions. Select the one that BEST answers the question or completes the statement. *PRINT THE LETTER OF THE CORRECT ANSWER IN THE SPACE AT THE RIGHT.*

1. A supplier quotes a list price of $172.00 less 15 and 10 percent for twelve tools. The actual cost for these twelve tools is MOST NEARLY

    A. $146   B. $132   C. $129   D. $112

    1._____

2. If the diameter of a circular piece of sheet metal is 1 1/2 feet, the area, in square inches, is MOST NEARLY

    A. 1.77   B. 2.36   C. 254   D. 324

    2._____

3. The sum of 5'6", 7'3", 9'3 1/2", and 3'7 1/4" is

    A. 19'8 1/2"   B. 22' 1/2"   C. 25'7 3/4"   D. 28'8 3/4"

    3._____

4. If the floor area of one shop is 15' by 21'3" and the size of an adjacent shop is 18' by 30'6", then the TOTAL floor area of these two shops is _____ square feet.

    A. 1127.75   B. 867.75   C. 549.0   D. 318.75

    4._____

5. The fraction which is equal to 0.875 is

    A. 7/16   B. 5/8   C. 3/4   D. 7/8

    5._____

6. The sum of 1/2, 2 1/32, 4 3/16, and 1 7/8 is MOST NEARLY

    A. 9.593   B. 9.625   C. 9.687   D. 10.593

    6._____

7. If the base of a right triangle is 9" and the altitude is 12", the length of the third side will be

    A. 13"   B. 14"   C. 15"   D. 16"

    7._____

8. If a steel bar 1" in diameter and 12' long weighs 32 lbs., then the weight of a piece of this bar 5'9" long is MOST NEARLY _____ lbs.

    A. 15.33   B. 15.26   C. 16.33   D. 15.06

    8._____

9. The diameter of a circle whose circumference is 12" is MOST NEARLY

    A. 3.82"   B. 3.72"   C. 3.62"   D. 3.52"

    9._____

10. A dimension of 39/64 inches converted to decimals is MOST NEARLY

    A. .600"   B. .609"   C. .607"   D. .611"

    10._____

11. A farm worker was paid a weekly wage of $415.20 for a 44-hour work week. As a result of a new labor contract, he is paid $431.40 a week for a 40-hour work week with time and one-half pay for time worked in excess of 40 hours in any work week.
    If he continues to work 44 hours weekly under the new contract, the amount by which his average hourly rate for a 44-hour work week under the new contract exceeds the hourly rate previously paid him lies between _____ and _____, inclusive.

    A. 80¢; $1.00 B. $1.00; $1.20
    C. $1.25; $1.45 D. $1.50; $1.70

12. The sum of 4 feet 3 1/4 inches, 7 feet 2 1/2 inches, and 11 feet 1/4 inch is _____ feet _____ inches.

    A. 21; 6 1/4   B. 22; 6   C. 23; 5   D. 24; 5 3/4

13. The number 0.038 is read as

    A. 38 tenths   B. 38 hundredths
    C. 38 thousandths   D. 38 ten-thousandths

14. Assume that an employee is paid at the rate of $10.86 per hour with time and a half for overtime past 40 hours in a week.
    If he works 43 hours in a week, his gross weekly pay is

    A. $434.40   B. $438.40   C. $459.18   D. $483.27

15. The sum of the following dimensions: 3'2 1/4", 8 7/8", 2'6 3/8", 2'9 3/4", and 1'0" is

    A. 16'7 1/4"   B. 10'7 1/4"   C. 10'3 1/4"   D. 9'3 1/4"

16. Two gears are meshed together and have a gear ratio of 6 to 1.
    If the small gear rotates 120 revolutions per minute, the large gear rotates at

    A. 20   B. 40   C. 60   D. 720

17. The vacuum side of a compound gage reads 14 inches of vacuum. The barometer reading is 29.76 inches of mercury. The equivalent absolute pressure of the compound gage reading, in inches of mercury, is MOST likely

    A. 15.06   B. 15.76   C. 43.06   D. 43.76

18. The fraction 5/8 expressed as a decimal is

    A. 0.125   B. 0.412   C. 0.625   D. 0.875

19. If 300 feet of a certain size pipe weighs 450 pounds, the number of pounds that 100 feet will weigh is

    A. 1,350   B. 150   C. 300   D. 250

20. As an oiler, you work for a facility that has automobiles that use, on the average, 600 quarts of one grade of lubricating oil every month.
    The number of one-gallon cans of the above oil that should be ordered each month to meet this requirement is

    A. 100   B. 125   C. 140   D. 150

21. The inside dimensions of a rectangular oil gravity tank are: height 15", width 9", length 10".
    The amount of oil in the tank, in gallons, (231 cu.in. = 1 gallon), when the oil level is 9" high, is MOST NEARLY

    A. 2.3 B. 3.5 C. 5.2 D. 5.8

22. If 30 gallons of oil cost $76.80, 45 gallons of oil at the same rate will cost

    A. $91.20 B. $115.20 C. $123.20 D. $131.20

23. If an oiler earns $18,000 in the first six months of a year and receives a 10% raise in salary for the next six months of the same year, his TOTAL earnings for the year will be

    A. $36,000 B. $37,500 C. $37,800 D. $39,600

24. If the cost of lubricating oil increases 15%, then a gallon of oil which used to cost $10.00 will now cost MOST NEARLY

    A. $10.50 B. $11.00 C. $11.50 D. $12.00

25. The sum of 7/8", 3/4", 1/2", and 3/8" is

    A. 2 1/8" B. 2 1/4" C. 2 3/8" D. 2 1/2"

KEY (CORRECT ANSWERS)

1. B
2. C
3. C
4. B
5. D

6. A
7. C
8. A
9. A
10. B

11. A
12. B
13. C
14. D
15. C

16. A
17. B
18. C
19. B
20. D

21. B
22. B
23. C
24. C
25. D

4 (#1)

SOLUTIONS TO PROBLEMS

1. Actual cost = ($172)(.85)(.90) = $131.58 ≈ $132

2. Radius = .75', then area = (3.14)(.75)^2 ≈ 1.77 sq.ft.
   Since 1 sq.ft. = 144 sq.in., the area ≈ 254 sq.in.

3. 5'6" + 7'3" + 9'3 1/2" + 3'7 1/4" = 24'19 3/4" = 25'7 3/4"

4. Total area = (15)(21.25) + (18)(30.5) = 867.75 sq.ft.

5. .875 = 875/1000 = 7/8

6. 1 1/2 + 2 1/32 + 4 3/16 + 1 7/8 = 8 51/32 = 9 19/32 = 9.593

7. Third side = $\sqrt{9^2+12^2} = \sqrt{225} = 15"$

8. Let x = weight. Then, 12/32 = 5.75/x . Solving, x ≈ 15.33 lbs.

9. 12" = (3.14)(diameter), so diameter ≈ 3.82"

10. $\frac{39}{64}$" = .609375" ≈ .609"

11. Under his new contract, the weekly wage for 44 hours can be found by first determining his hourly rate for the first 40 hours = $431.40 ÷ 40 ≈ $10.80. Now, his time and one-half pay will = ($10.80)(1.5) = $16.20. His weekly wage for the new contract = $431.40 + (4)($16.20) = $496.20. His new hourly rate for 44 hours = $496.20 ÷ 44 ≈ $10.34. Under the old contract, his hourly rate for 44 hours was $415.20 ÷ 44 = $9.44. His hourly rate increase = $10.34 - $9.44 = $0.90. (Answer key: between $0.80 and $1.00)

12. 4'3 1/4" + 7'2 1/2" + 11' 1/4" = 22'6"

13. .038 = 38 thousandths

14. ($10.86)(40) + ($16.29)(3) = $483.27

15. 3'2 1/4" + 8 7/8" + 2'6 3/8" + 2'9 3/4" + 1'0" = 8'25 18/8" = 10'3 1/4"

16. The gear ratio is inversely proportional to the gear size. Let x = large gear's rpm. Then, 6/1 = 120/x . Solving, x = 20

17. Subtract 14 from 29.76

18. 5/8 = .625

19. Let x = number of pounds. Then, 300/450 = 100/x . Solving, x = 150

20. 600 quarts = 150 gallons, since 4 quarts = 1 gallon

21. (9")(9")(10") = 810 cu.in. Then, 810 ÷ 231 ≈ 3.5

22. Let x = unknown cost. Then, 30/$76.80 = 45/x. Solving, x = $115.20

23. $18,000 + ($18,000)(1.10) = $37,800

24. ($10.00)(1.15) = $11.50

25. 7/8" + 3/4" + 1/2" + 3/8" = 20/8" = 2 1/2"

TEST 2

DIRECTIONS: Each question or incomplete statement is followed by several suggested answers or completions. Select the one that BEST answers the question or completes the statement. *PRINT THE LETTER OF THE CORRECT ANSWER IN THE SPACE AT THE RIGHT.*

1. A sheet metal plate has been cut in the form of a right triangle with sides of 5, 12, and 13 inches.
   The area of this plate, in square inches, is

   A. 30 B. 32 1/2 C. 60 D. 78

   1.____

2. If steel weighs 480 lbs. per cubic foot, the weight of an 18" x 18" x 2" steel base plate is _____ lbs.

   A. 180 B. 216 C. 427 D. 648

   2.____

3. By trial, it is found that by using 2 cubic feet of sand, a 5 cubic foot batch of concrete is produced.
   Using the same proportions, the amount of sand, in cubic feet, required to produce 2 cubic yards of concrete is MOST NEARLY

   A. 7 B. 22 C. 27 D. 45

   3.____

4. The total number of cubic yards of earth to be removed to make a trench 3'9" wide, 25'0" long, and 4'3" deep is MOST NEARLY

   A. 53.1 B. 35.4 C. 26.6 D. 14.8

   4.____

5. A large number of 2 x 4 studs, some 10'5" long and some 6'5 1/2" long, are required for a job.
   To minimize waste, it would be PREFERABLE to order lengths of _____ feet.

   A. 16 B. 17 C. 18 D. 19

   5.____

6. A 6" pipe is connected to a 4" pipe through a reducer. If 100 cubic feet of water is flowing through the 6" pipe per minute, the flow, in cubic feet, per minute through the 4" pipe is

   A. 225 B. 100 C. 66.6 D. 44.4

   6.____

7. If steel weighs 0.28 pounds per cubic inch, then the weight, in pounds, of a 2" square steel bar 120" long is MOST NEARLY

   A. 115 B. 125 C. 135 D. 155

   7.____

8. A three-inch diameter steel bar two feet long weighs MOST NEARLY (assume steel weighs 480 lbs./cu.ft.) _____ lbs.

   A. 48 B. 58 C. 68 D. 78

   8.____

9. The area of a circular plate will be reduced by 5% if a sector removed from it has an angle of _____ degrees.

   A. 18 B. 24 C. 32 D. 60

   9.____

10. If a 4 1/16 inch shaft wears six thousandths of an inch, the NEW diameter will be _____ inches.

    A. 4.0031   B. 4.0565   C. 4.0578   D. 4.0605

11. A set of mechanical plan drawings is drawn to a scale of 1/8" = 1 foot.
    If a length of pipe measures 15 7/16" on the drawing, the ACTUAL length of the pipe is _____ feet.

    A. 121.5   B. 122.5   C. 123.5   D. 124.5

12. An electrical drawing is drawn to a scale of 1/4" = 1'. If a length of conduit on the drawing measures 7 3/8", the actual length of the conduit, in feet, is

    A. 7.5   B. 15.5   C. 22.5   D. 29.5

13. Assume that you have assigned 6 mechanics to do a job that must be finished in 4 days. At the end of 3 days, your men have completed only two-thirds of the job. In order to complete the job on time and because the job is such that it cannot be speeded up, you should assign a MINIMUM of _____ extra men.

    A. 3   B. 4   C. 5   D. 6

14. Assume that a trench is 42" wide, 5' deep, and 100' long. If the unit price of excavating the trench is $105 per cubic yard, the cost of excavating the trench is MOST NEARLY

    A. $6,805   B. $15,330   C. $21,000   D. $63,000

15. If the scale on a shop drawing is 1/4 inch to the foot, then the length of a part which measures 2 3/8 inches long on the drawing is ACTUALLY _____ feet.

    A. 9 1/2   B. 8 1/2   C. 7 1/4   D. 4 1/4

16. It is necessary to pour a new concrete floor for a shop. If the dimensions of the concrete slab for the floor are to be 27' x 18' x 6", then the number of cubic yards of concrete that must be poured is

    A. 9   B. 16   C. 54   D. 243

17. The jaws of a vise move 1/4" for each complete turn of the handle.
    The number of complete turns necessary to open the jaws 2 3/4" is

    A. 9   B. 10   C. 11   D. 12

18. Assume that a jobbing shop is to submit a price for a contract involving 300 pieces of work. Assume that material costs 50 cents per piece, labor costs $7.50 an hour, and a lathe operator can complete 5 pieces in an hour.
    If overhead is 40% of material and labor costs and the profit is 10% of all costs, the submitted price for the entire job will be

    A. $630.24   B. $872.80   C. $900.00   D. $924.00

19. The following formula is used in connection with the three-wire method of measuring pitch diameters of screw threads: $G = \dfrac{0.57735}{N}$, where G = wire size and N = number of threads per inch.
According to this formula, the proper size of wire for a 1"-8NC thread is MOST NEARLY

   A. .0722"   B. .7217"   C. .0072"   D. .0074"

20. A millimeter is 1/25.4 of an inch and there are 10 millimeters to a centimeter.
If a piece of stock measures 127 centimeters long, the length of the stock, in feet and inches, would be MOST NEARLY

   A. 2'1"   B. 4'2"   C. 8'4"   D. 41'8"

21. For a certain job, you will need 25 steel bars 1 inch in diameter and 4"6" long.
If these bars weigh 3 pounds per foot of length, then the TOTAL weight for all 25 bars is _____ pounds.

   A. 13.5   B. 75.0   C. 112.5   D. 337.5

22. If steel weighs 0.30 pounds per cubic inch, then the weight of a 2 inch square steel bar 90 inches long is _____ pounds.

   A. 27   B. 54   C. 108   D. 360

23. A concrete wall is 36' long, 9' high, and 1 1/2' thick. The number of cubic yards of concrete that were needed to make this wall is

   A. 14   B. 18   C. 27   D. 36

24. If the scale on a shop drawing is 1/2 inch to the foot, then the length of a part which measures 41/4 inches long on the drawing has a length of APPROXIMATELY _____ feet.

   A. 2 1/8   B. 4 1/4   C. 8 1/2   D. 10 3/4

25. If the allowable load on a wooden scaffold is 60 pounds per square foot and the scaffold surface area is 3 feet by 12 feet, then the MAXIMUM total distributed load that is permitted on the scaffold is _____ pounds.

   A. 720   B. 1,800   C. 2,160   D. 2,400

KEY (CORRECT ANSWERS)

1. A
2. A
3. B
4. D
5. B

6. B
7. C
8. A
9. A
10. B

11. C
12. D
13. A
14. A
15. A

16. A
17. C
18. D
19. A
20. B

21. D
22. C
23. B
24. C
25. C

SOLUTIONS TO PROBLEMS

1. Area = (1/2)(base)(height) = (1/2)(5")(12") = 30 sq.in.

2. Volume = (18") (18") (2") = 648 cu.in. = 648/1720 cu.ft.
   Then, (480)(648/1720) = ≈ 180 lbs.

3. 2 cu.yds. = 54 cu.ft. Let x = required cubic feet of sand. Then, 2/5 = x/54. Solving, x = 21.6 (or about 22)

4. (3.75')(25')(4.25') = 398.4375 cu.ft. ≈ 14.8 cu.yds.

5. 10'5" + 6'5 1/2" = 16'10 1/2", so lengths of 17 feet are needed

6. The amount of water flowing through each pipe must be equal.

7. (2")(2")(120") = 480 cu. in. Then, (480)(.28) ≈ 135 lbs.

8. Volume = $(\pi)(.125')^2(2)$ ≈ .1 cu.ft. Then, (.1)(480) = 48 lbs.

9. (360°)(.05) - 18°

10. 4 1/16 - .006 = 4.0625 - .006 = 4.0565

11. 15 7/16" ÷ 1/8" = 247/16 . 8/1 = 123.5. Then, (123.5)(1 ft.) = 123.5 ft.

12. 7 3/8" ÷ 1/4" = 59/8 . 4/1 = 29.5 Then, (29.5)(1 ft.) = 29.5 ft.

13. (6)(4) = 24 man-days normally required. Since after 3 days only the equivalent of (2/3)(24) = 16 man-days of work has been 1 done, 8 man-days of work is still left. 16 ÷ 3 = 5 1/3, which means the crew is equivalent to only 5 1/3 men. To do the 8 man-days of work, it will require at least 8 - 5 1/3 = 2 2/3 = 3 additional men.

14. (3.5')(5')(100') = 1750 cu.ft. ≈ 64.8 cu.yds. Then, (64.8)($105) ≈ $6805

15. 2 3/8" ÷ 1/4" = 19/8 . 4/1 = 9 1/2 Then, (9 1/2)(1 ft.) = 9 1/2 feet

16. (27')(18')(1/2') = 243 cu.ft. = 9 cu.yds. (1 cu.yd. = 27 cu.ft.)

17. 2 3/4" ÷ 1/4" = 11/4 . 4/1 = 11

18. Material cost = (300)($.50) = $150. Labor cost = ($7.50)(300/5) = $450. Overhead = (.40)($150+$450) = $240. Profit = .10($150+$450+$240) = $84. Submitted price = $150 + $450 + $240 + $84 = $924

19. 6 = .57735" ÷ 8 = .0722"

20. 127 cm = 1270 mm = 1270/25.4" ≈ 50" = 4.2"

21. (25)(4.5') = 112.5' Then, (112.5X3) = 337.5 lbs.

22. (2")(2")(90") = 360 cu.in. Then, (360)(30) = 108 lbs.

23. (36')(9')(1 1/2') = 486 cu.ft. = 18 cu.yds. (1 cu.yd. = 27 cu.ft.)

24. 4 1/4" ÷ 1/2" = 17/4 . 2/1 = 8 1/2. Then, (8 1/2)(1 ft.) = 8 1/2 ft.

25. (12')(3') = 36 sq.ft. Then, (36)(60) = 2160 lbs.

———

TEST 3

DIRECTIONS: Each question or incomplete statement is followed by several suggested answers or completions. Select the one that BEST answers the question or completes the statement. *PRINT THE LETTER OF THE CORRECT ANSWER IN THE SPACE AT THE RIGHT.*

1. A right triangular metal sheet for a roofing job has sides of 36 inches and 4 feet. The length of the remaining side is

    A. 7 feet
    B. 6 feet
    C. 60 inches
    D. 90 inches

2. A U.S. Standard Gauge thickness is given as 0.15625. This thickness, in fractions of an inch, is MOST NEARLY _____ inches.

    A. 1/8   B. 4/32   C. 5/32   D. 3/64

3. The weight per 100 of sheet metal fasteners is given as 2/3 pound. The APPROXIMATE number of fasteners in a 2-pound package is

    A. 166   B. 200   C. 300   D. 266

4. The decimal equivalent of 27/32 is MOST NEARLY

    A. 0.813   B. 0.828   C. 0.844   D. 0.859

5. If a scaled measurement of 1'3" on the drawing of a sheet metal layout represents an actual length of 10'0", then the drawing has been made to a scale of _____ inch to the foot.

    A. 3/4   B. 1 1/4   C. 1 1/2   D. 1 3/4

6. Two and two-thirds tees can be made from one sheet of steel. If 24 tees must be made, then the number of sheets required is

    A. 6   B. 7   C. 8   D. 9

7. A main duct 20 inches in diameter discharges into two branch ducts. The sum of the areas of the branches is to be equal to the area of the main duct. One branch is 12 inches in diameter.
The diameter of the other branch is _____ inches.

    A. 16   B. 12   C. 10   D. 8

8. If steel weighs 480 lbs. per cubic foot, the weight of 10 sheets, each 6 feet by 3 feet by 1/32 inch, is _____ lbs.

    A. 2,700   B. 1,237   C. 270   D. 225

9. The area, in square inches, of a right triangle that has sides of 12 1/2, 10, and 7 1/2 inches is

    A. 18 1/4   B. 37 1/2   C. 75   D. 60

10. In making a container to hold 1 gallon (231 cu.in.) and to be 6 inches in diameter at the top and 8 inches in diameter at the bottom, the height must be, in inches,

    A. 10.0 B. 8.2 C. 4.6 D. 6

11. A sheet metal worker is given a job to make a transition piece from a 8 1/2" diameter duct to an 11 1/4" diameter duct. If the length of the transition piece is 5 1/2" for each inch change in diameter, then the length of the transition piece is

    A. 14 7/8" B. 15" C. 15 1/8" D. 15 1/4"

12. A duct layout is drawn to a scale of 3/8" to a foot. If the length of a run shown on the drawing scales 7 1/2", then the ACTUAL length of the run is

    A. 19'6" B. 19'9" C. 20'0" D. 20'3"

13. An 18" x 24" duct is to be connected to a 24" x 24" duct by means of an eccentric transition piece (3 sides flush). If the taper is to be 1" in 4", then the length of the transition piece is

    A. 6" B. 12" C. 18" D. 24"

14. Twenty-seven pairs of 3/8" diameter rods each 3'3 1/2" long are needed to support a duct.
    If the available rods are ten feet long, then the MINIMUM number of rods that will be needed to make the twenty-seven sets is

    A. 9 B. 12 C. 15 D. 18

15. A rectangular sheet metal air duct with open ends is 12 feet long and 15" x 20" in cross-section. If one square foot of the sheet metal weighs 1/2 pound, then the TOTAL weight of the duct is _____ lbs.

    A. 10 B. 17 1/2 C. 35 D. 150

16. The sum of 1/12 and 1/4 is

    A. 1/3 B. 5/12 C. 7/12 D. 3/8

17. The product of 12 and 2 1/3 is

    A. 27 B. 28 C. 29 D. 30

18. If 4 1/2 is subtracted from 7 1/5, the remainder is

    A. 3 7/10 B. 2 7/10 C. 3 3/10 D. 2 3/10

19. The number of cubic yards in 47 cubic feet is MOST NEARLY

    A. 1.70 B. 1.74 C. 1.78 D. 1.82

20. A wall 8'0" high by 12'6" long has a window opening 4'0" high by 3'6" wide. The net area of the wall (allowing for the window opening) is, in square feet,

    A. 86 B. 87 C. 88 D. 89

21. A worker's hourly rate is $11.36. If he works 11 1/2 hours, he should receive

 A. $129.84 B. $130.64 C. $131.48 D. $132.24

22. The number of cubic feet in 3 cubic yards is

 A. 81 B. 82 C. 83 D. 84

23. At an annual rate of $.40 per $100, what is the fire insurance premium for one year on a house that is insured for $80,000?

 A. $120 B. $160 C. $240 D. $320

24. A meter equals approximately 1.09 yards. How much longer, in yards, is a 100-meter dash than a 100-yard dash?

 A. 6 B. 8 C. 9 D. 12

25. A train leaves New York City at 8:10 A.M. and arrives in Buffalo at 4:45 P.M. on the same day. How long, in hours and minutes, does it take the train to make the trip? _____ hours, _____ minutes.

 A. 6; 22 B. 7; 16 C. 7; 28 D. 8; 35

KEY (CORRECT ANSWERS)

1. C   11. C
2. C   12. C
3. C   13. D
4. C   14. D
5. C   15. C

6. D   16. A
7. A   17. B
8. D   18. B
9. B   19. B
10. D   20. A

21. B
22. A
23. D
24. C
25. D

SOLUTIONS TO PROBLEMS

1. Let x = remaining side. Converting to inches, $x^2 = 36^2 + 48^2$ So, $x^2 = 3600$. Solving, x = 60 inches.

2. $.15625 = \dfrac{15,625}{100,000} = \dfrac{5}{32}$

3. 2 ÷ 2/3 = 3. Then, (3)(100) = 300 fasteners

4. 27/32 = .84375 ≈ .844

5. 1'3" ÷ 10 = 15" ÷ 10 = 1 1/2"

6. 24 ÷ 2 2/3 = 24/1.3/8 = 9

7. Area of main duct = $(\pi)(10^2) = 100\pi$. One of the branches has an area of $(\pi)(6^2) = 36\pi$. Thus, the area of the 2nd branch = $100\pi - 36\pi = 64\pi$. The 2nd branch's radius must be 8" and its diameter must be 16".

8. Volume = (1/384')(6')(3') = .046875 cu.ft. Then, 10 sheets have a volume of .46875 cu.ft. Now, (.46875)(480) = 225 lbs.

9. Note that $(7\ 1/2)^2 + (10)^2 = (12\ 1/2)^2$, so that this is a right triangle. Area = (1/2)(10")(7 1/2") = 37 1/2 sq.in.

10. $231 = \dfrac{h}{3}[(\pi)(3)^2 + (\pi)(4)^2 + \sqrt{(9\pi)(16\pi)}]$, where h = required height. Then,

    $231 = \dfrac{h}{3}(9\pi + 16\pi + 12\pi)$. Simplifying, $231 = 37\pi h/3$.
    Solving, h ~ 5.96" or 6"

11. 11 1/4 - 8 1/2 = 2 3/4. Then, (2 3/4)(5 1/2) = 11/4 .11/2 = 15 1/8

12. 7 1/2" ÷ 3/8" = 15/2 .8/3 = 20 Then, (20)(1 ft.) = 20 feet

13. 24" - 18" = 6" Then, (6")(4) = 24"

14. 3'3 1/2" = 39.5". Now, (27)(2)(39.5") = 2133". 10 ft. = 120".
    Finally, 2133 ÷ 120 = 17.775, so 18 rods are needed.

15. Surface area = (2)(12')(1 1/4') + (2)(12')(1 2/3') = 70 sq.ft.
    Then, (70)(1/2 lb.) - 35 lbs.

16. 1/12 + 1/4 = 4/12 = 1/3

17. (12)(2 1/3) = 12/1 . 7/3 = 28

18. 7 1/5 - 4 1/2 = 7 2/10 - 4 5/10 = 6 12/10 - 4 5/10 = 2 7/10

19. 47 cu.ft. = 47/27 cu.yds. = 1.74 cu.yds.

20. (8')(12.5') - (4')(3.5') = 86 sq.ft.

21. ($11.36)(11.5) = $130.64

22. 1 cu.yd. = 27 cu.ft., so 3 cu.yds. = 81 cu.ft.

23. $80,000 ÷ $100 = 800. Then, (800)($.40) = $320

24. 100 meters = 109 yds. Then, 109 - 100 = 9 yds.

25. 4:45 P.M. - 8:10 AM. = 8 hrs. 35 min.

GLOSSARY OF METAL WORKING

CONTENTS

	Page
Abrasive ...... Base Metal	1
Bastard ...... Brass	2
Brass Bound ...... Cadmium	3
Calipers ...... Cobolt	4
Cold Chisel ...... Drift	5
Drill Bit ...... Fish Plate	6
Flaring ...... Gunmetal	7
Hacksaw ...... Hollowing Hammer	8
Iron ...... Malleable	9
Mallet ...... Ore	10
Oxidation or Oxidization ...... Post vise	11
Pumice ...... Rust	12
Safe Edge ...... Smooth cut	13
Snap head ...... Steel sheet	14
Stock ...... Tinner's or Tinman's Solder	15
Tinning ...... Wing nut	16
Wiped joint ...... Zinc Chloride	17
Properties of Metals	18
Properties of Alloys	18
Soldering Fluxes	19
Composition of Some Alloys	19

GLOSSARY OF METAL WORKING

A

ABRASIVE
A natural or artificial substance used for grinding, polishing, buffing, lapping or sandblasting. Commonly includes garnet, emery, corundum, diamond, aluminum oxide and silicon carbide.

ACID PICKLE
Diluted acid used for cleaning metal.

AGE HARDEN
The capacity of some metals to get harder as they get older.

ALLOY
A substance having metallic qualities, composed of one or more chemical elements, at least one of which is a metallic element.

ALUMINUM
Lightweight soft white-colored metal, usually alloyed with other metals to increase its hardness and other qualities.

ANGLE IRON
Mild steel. Bars with 90 degree cross-section.

ANNEALING
Treating metal to make it as soft as possible (usually by heating and cooling slowly). The necessary technique varies between metals and alloys.

ANODIZING
Chemical surface treatment for protection and decoration of aluminum and its alloys.

ANTIQUEING
Darkening copper or brass by chemical treatment.

ASBESTOS
Fibrous silicate mineral that is incombustible.

ASH
Springy hard wood used for hammer and mallet handles.

B

BALL PEIN
Hemispherical end of a hammer head.

BASE METAL
At one time, the name for common metals. They are contrast to the "noble" metals which are valuable.

BASTARD
A grade of fairly coarse file.

BEAK OR BICK
Round conical end of an anvil or stake. Also horn.

BELL MOUTH
Spread end of tube.

BICK IRON
Light anvil for sheet metalwork.

BIT
Jaws of tongs. A drill.

BLIND RIVETING
Using tubular rivets on a mandrel with a device for closing each rivet from one side of the metal.

BLOCKING HAMMER
A hammer with two large flat faces.

BLOWLAMP
A torch burning gas, kerosene or other fuel to produce a flame in the form of a jet.

BOLSTER
Block with hole to support work being punched.

BOLT
Screw fastening with a head to take a nut. Only threaded part of its length. If it is threaded fully to its head, it is a metal-threaded screw.

BORAX
Flux for hard soldering and brazing.

BOSS
Center part of a wheel. A locally raised part of sheet metal. The punch used to raise it.

BOSSING MALLET
Wooden mallet with an egg-shaped head for shaping sheet metal.

BOUGE
Knock out dents in raised work over a stake.

BRAKE
Mechanical device for folding sheet metal.

BRASS
An alloy consisting mainly of copper and zinc to which small amounts of other metals may be added. Common brass is yellow.

BRASS-BOUND
Strengthened with brass straps. Particularly a wooden box or chest.

BRASS SCRIBER
Pointed brass rod used to mark tinplate.

BRASS TONGS
Tongs for dipping non-ferrous metals in acid pickles.

BRAZING
Joining by melting spelter or hard solder.

BRAZING HEARTH
Trough to hold coke or asbestos and support work while it is brazed.

BRONZE
Copper alloy with tin and other metals.

BRONZE AGE
Early period after the Stone Age when primitive man made tools and implements from an early form of copper alloy.

BUFF
To polish the surface of metal with a powered buffing wheel.

BUFFING WHEEL
Fabric disks held together, usually by sewing, forming a wheel to be rotated at high speed and used for polishing. Also called a polishing mop.

BURIN
An engraving tool.

BURNISHER
Hard steel rubbing tool. Shaping tool used in metal spinning.

BURR
Turned over edge. Small rotary file.

BUTTERFLY NUT
A nut to fit on a bolt with projections for hand tightening. Also a wing nut.

BUTT STRAP
Riveted strip over meeting edges. Also a fish plate.

<u>C</u>

CADMIUM
Metal used for plating steel to protect it from corrosion.

CALIPERS
Tool with hinged curved jaws for checking thickness and diameters.

CANISTER STAKE
Cylindrical stake with a flat end.

CARBIDE TIP
A very hard tip to make a cutting edge bonded to tool steel, using carbide, which is a compound of carbon with one or more metallic elements.

CARBON
Element added to iron to make steel.

CARRIAGE BOLT
Bolt with a shallow domed head and square neck to prevent it from turning in wood.

CARRIAGE SCREW
A large wood screw with a head to take to wrench.

CASTING
Melting metal and pouring it into molds.

CENTER PUNCH
Pointed punch to make a dot in metal.

CENTIGRADE or CELSIUS
Temperature scale with the freezing point of water 0 degrees and the boiling point 100 degrees.

CHALK LINE
Fine cord that is used with chalk to strike a line.

CHATTER MARKS
Ridges produced by vibration during filing or other work.

CHISEL
An end-cutting tool for wood or metal.

CHROMIUM
Metal that can be alloyed with steel or used for plating.

CHUCK
A holding device for a drill or a lathe. A former for metal spinning.

CIRCUMFERENCE
Distance around a circle or other rounded shape. A similar distance around an angular shape is a perimeter.

COBOLT
Rare metal which can be added to steel to increase its magnetic properties.

COLD CHISEL
A tool that is hammered for cutting cold metal.

CORROSION
Oxidization of the surface of metal such as rust on iron.

CORRUGATED IRON
Sheet iron or steel ridged and grooved regularly across its width. It is usually protected by galvanizing.

COPPER
Red colored non-ferrous metal.

COUNTERSINK
Bevelled edge of hole. The tool for doing this.

CREASING HAMMER
A hammer with two narrow cross peins.

CREASING IRON
Stake with grooves across.

CROCUS
Fine polishing powder.

CURVE ALLOWANCE
Size correction at a bend due to measuring around the neutral axis.

<u>D</u>

DEVELOPMENT
Outline of the shape while metal is flat that will give the desired shape after bending.

DIAMETER
Distance across a circle.

DIE
Tool for cutting a screw thread on a rod. A form into which metal is pressed for shaping.

DIVIDERS
Hinged pair of points for scratching a circle or comparing distances

DRAW FILLING
Using a file sideways along an edge to remove cross file marks.

DRAWING
Pulling metal through holes to form wire.

DRIFT
Punch used to draw holes into line.

DRILL BIT
Tool for making a hole by cutting (as distinct from punching).

DRILL PRESS
A machine which uses drill bits to make holes.

E

ELEMENT
Any of about 100 substances that cannot be revolved by chemical means into simpler substances.

EMBOSS
Raise sheet metal, with a hammer, punch or boss from the reverse side.

EMERY
Grit used as abrasive on metal.

ESCUTCHEON
Key hole or the plate around it.

ETCHING
Eating into metal with acid to produce a design, usually a name.

EXCRUDING
Forcing metal through a die to form rods of special section.

EYE BOLT
Bolt with flattened or shaped end with a hole through.

F

FAHRENHEIT
Common temperature scale.

FERROUS
Alloy containing iron.

FERRULE
A tube or cap on a wooden handle to prevent it from splitting.

FILE
Tool with teeth made with grooves cut across it.

FILE CARD
Wire brush for cleaning files.

FISH PLATE
Alternative name for butt strap.

FLARING
　　Spreading the end of a tube. Giving it a bell mouth.

FLANGE
　　Folded edge.

FLASH
　　The movement of solder as it melts around a joint. Excess solder to be removed.

FLUX
　　Liquid or powder used to help a metal or an alloy to flow in welding, brazing or soldering.

FOCUS
　　Plural is foci. Point about which a curved shape is generated, The center of a circle is its focus. An ellipse has two foci.

FOLDING BARS
　　Parallel bars used for bending sheet metal.

<u>G</u>

GALVANIZED IRON
　　Iron coated with zinc as a protection against rust.

GAUGE
　　Size, particularly the thickness of sheets or the diameter of wires, according to a recognized scale. The tool for measuring this.

GILDING
　　Coating with gold leaf.

GILDING METAL
　　Alloy of copper and zinc with a greater proportion of copper than in brass.

GOLD
　　One of the rare or noble metals.

GRAVER
　　Cutting tool with a diamond-shaped cutting point.

GROOVING STAKE
　　Alternative name for a creasing iron.

GUILLOTINE
　　Large mechanical shearing machine.

GUNMETAL
　　Alloy of copper and tin.

H

HACKSAW
Metal-cutting handsaw with its blade tensioned in a frame.

HALF-MOON STAKE
A hatchet stake with a curved edge.

HARD SOLDER
Copper/zinc alloy with other metals added to lower its melting point.

HATCHET SOLDERING IRON
An iron with a copper bit at an angle to the shaft and a straight thin edge.

HATCHET STAKE
Stake with straight sharp edge for bending sheet metal across its top.

HEARTH
Any container for coke or other solid fuel.

HEAT TREATMENT
Heating steel to alter its character. This includes annealing, hardening, tempering and normalizing. Annealing other metals by heating.

HEEL
Opposite end of anvil or bick iron to the beak.

HICKORY
Springy wood used for mallet and hammer handles.

HIDE MALLET
A mallet with a head formed from rolled leather.

HIGH CARBON STEEL
Steel with sufficient carbon to permit hardening and tempering.

HOLD UP
Support one rivet head while the other is formed.

HOLLOW GROUND
A concave bevel on a cutting edge.

HONING
Sharpening or smoothing with a fine abrasive stone.

HORN
Alternative name for beak of anvil or bick iron.

HOLLOWING HAMMER
A hammer with two ball peins.

I

IRON
Silver-white common metal which can be alloyed with carbon to make steel.

IRON AGE
A prehistoric age when man first learned how to make tools and weapons from iron.

J

JAWS
Gripping surfaces of tongs or vise.

JENNY
Hand-operated machine for flanging and wiring sheet metal edges.

K

KILLED SPIRITS
Zinc chloride used as flux when soldering.

L

LEAD
Heavy and soft grey metal. The amount a nut moves forward in one revolution on a threaded rod.

LEG VISE
A strong vise attached to a bench, but with a leg extending to the floor.

LOW CARBON STEEL
Steel that does not contain the proper amount of carbon to permit tempering. Also called mild steel.

M

MACHINIST'S VISE
Vise with a parallel action to mount on a bench.

MAGNESIUM
Very light and combustible metal.

MALACCA
Species of cane used for mallot handles.

MALL OR MAUL
Large two-handed mallet.

MALLEABLE
Capable of being shaped.

MALLET
Type of hammer with wood, rawhide or plastic head.

MANDREL OR MANDRIL
Iron block on which parts are shaped. Particularly a round cone for shaping rings.

MEAN
Average or center. A mean line is the center of the thickness of bent sheet metal.

MILD STEEL
Low-carbon steel which cannot be tempered.

METALLURGY
The science and technology of metals.

MICROMETER
Instrument for making fine measurements using the rotation of a screw.

MUSHROOM STAKE
A round-topped steel anvil.

N

NEUTRAL AXIS
The mean line in the thickness of metal that is neither stretched nor compressed when it is bent.

NIBBLER
Shearing tool that removes particles along a line.

NICKEL
Metal alloyed with steel and used for plating.

NOBLE METALS
At one time the name for valuable metals in contrast with the "base" metals.

NON-FERROUS
Alloy that does not contain iron.

NORMALIZE
Reduce internal stresses after working by heating and allowing to cool slowly in the same way as annealing steel.

O

OFFSET
Double bend to alter alignment of a bar or sheet.

ORE
Solid naturally occurring mineral aggregate from which metal is extracted.

OXIDATION OR OXIDIZATION
　　The effect of air on the surface of metal.

P

PATINA
　　Colored oxidation on metal surfaces due to long exposure to air particularly on bronze. It can be simulated by chemical action.

PEEN, PEIN or PANE
　　The shaped end of a hammer head.

PEENING
　　Hollowing with ball peen hammer.

PERIMETER
　　Distance around an angular outline. A similar measurement around a curve is a circumference.

PICKLE
　　Dilute acid for cleaning metals.

PIERCING
　　Cutting internal fretted shapes in sheet metal with a fine saw in a frame.

PITCH
　　Composition for supporting repousse work. Distance between holes or the tops of a screw thread.

PLANISHING
　　Hammering all over to harden and decorate.

PLANISHING HAMMER
　　A hammer with highly polished flat or domed faces.

PLATE
　　Alternative name for sheet metal. Usually of the thickert types.

PLATINUM
　　Rare and valuable metal used especially in jewelry.

PLIERS
　　Small gripping tool with tongs action.

POP RIVETING
　　Alternative name for blind riveting.

POST VISE
　　Alternative name for a leg vise.

PUMICE
Volcanic powder used as a fine abrasive.

PUNCH
Tool intended to be hit with a hammer to make a dent or hole.

Q

QUENCH
To cool hot metal quickly in a liquid.

R

RADIUS
Distance from the center to the circumference of a circle.

RAISING
Making a deep bowl shape by hammering over a stake.

RAISING HAMMER
A hammer with two cross peins.

RASP
A coarse file type of tool with teeth individually raised.

RAKE
Cutting angle of a drill or other tool.

REPOUSSÉ
Method of raising a pattern from the back of thin metal.

REPOUSSÉ HAMMER
Light hammer with broad-faced pein.

ROLLING
Squeezing metal between rollers to form sheets.

ROUGE
Fine polishing powder.

ROUT
Cut grooves or hollows.

RULE
Measuring tool. Not "ruler."

RUST
Corrosion on iron steel.

S

SAFE EDGE
One edge of a file without teeth. Turned-in edge of sheet metal,

SAND BAG
Leather bag containing sand on which hollowing is done.

SATE
Alternative name for a sett. Used to flatten metal.

SCALLOP
An evenly waved edge.

SCREW
A fastening to take a nut that threaded to the head. If it is only threaded part way, it is a bolt. A screw can cut its own thread in wood or sheet metal.

SCOTS SHEARS
Large snips.

SCRIBE OR SCRIBER
Hard sharp steel point for scratching metal.

SECOND CUT
The grade of file commonly used on edges of sheet metal.

SELF-TAPPING SCREW
Hardened steel screw that cuts its thread in sheet metal.

SET
A hammer-like head on a wooden handle that is hit with a hammer to shape metal.

SET SCREW
Screw used to draw parts together.

SHANK
The neck or part of a tool between the handle and the blade.

SHEAR
Large snips that are often bench mounted with a lever handle.

SILVER SOLDER
Copper/zinc alloy with a small amount of silver included to lower its melting point.

SLEDGE
A large two-handed hammer.

SMOOTH CUT
The finest grade file normally used.

SNAP HEAD
Raised round head on a rivet.

SNIPS
Scissor action shears for cutting sheet metal.

SOFT SOLDER
Low melting point solder. A lead/tin alloy.

SOLDER
Alloy used to fuse into joints. The action of soldering.

SOLDERING IRON
Tool with copper bit that is heated to melt solder.

SPATULA
Iron rod with flattened end that is used to place flux and spelter in brazing or for hard soldering.

SPELTER
Form of brass used in brazing.

SPINNING
Shaping sheet metal in a lathe.

SPRING STEEL
High carbon steel that is similar to tool steel.

SQUARE
As a setting out term, this means at right angles.

STAINLESS STEEL
Steel alloyed with other metals to resist corrosion.

STAKE
Shaped block used as an anvil in sheet metalwork.

STAKE VISE
Alternative name for leg vise.

STEEL
Alloy of iron and carbon.

STEEL PLATE
Steel rolled into sheets more than about three-sixteenths of an inch thick.

STEEL SHEET
Steel rolled thinner than steel plate.

STOCK
Supply of metal. The body of a tool. One head of a lathe.

STRIKE A LINE
Draw a line using a chalked cord.

STROP
Leather strap used in the final stages of tool sharpening.

SULFURIC ACID
Corrosive fluid used in cleaning metal.

SWAGE BLOCK
Large block with many hollows and holes.

SWARF
Filings and other waste removed from metal.

T

TAIL
Oppposite end of anvil or bick iron to the beak. Also heel.

TANG
Part of a tool that is driven into a handle.

TAP
Tool for cutting a screw thread in a hole.

TEMPER
Reduced full hardened steel to a lesser hardness and less brittle form for a particular use.

TEMPLATE or TEMPLET
Pattern used for marking around to transfer an outline.

THREE-SQUARE FILE
A file with a triangular cross section.

TIN
White metal used in alloys and for coating steel for protection against corrosion.

TINMAN'S or TINNER'S MALLET
Mallet with a cylindrical wood head.

TINNER
Worker in tinplate.

TINNER'S or TINMAN'S SOLDER
Lead/tin alloy. Also called soft solder.

TINNING
In soldering, coating the bit or the surfaces to be joined with soft solder,

TINPLATE
Thin sheet steel that is coated with tin.

TINSNIPS
Small shears for cutting sheet metal.

TINSMITH
Alternative name for tinner or tinman.

TORCH
Device for burning gas to produce a forced flame that can be adjusted to size.

TRACER
Narrow-ended punch used for decorative lines.

TRAMMEL HEADS
Sliding heads on a bar for use as large compasses or dividers.

TRIPOLI
A fine polishing compound.

TRUNCATED
Cut off. Usually applied to part of a cone.

V

VISE
Two-jawed device with a tightening screw. Attached to bench and used to hold metal being worked on.

VISE GRIP PLIERS
Pliers that can be locked on to the work.

VISE CLAMPS
Sheet metal covers that are placed over vise jaws.

W

WELD
Fuse two pieces of metal together with heat.

WHITING
Powder used for polishing tinplate.

WING NUT
Alternative name for butterfly nut.

WIPED JOINT
　　Joint between pipes made with plumber's solder.

WIRE EDGE
　　Burr on the edge of a sharpened tool.

WIRED EDGE
　　Wire enclosed in a rolled sheet metal edge.

WORK HARDEN
　　Hardening due to hammering or other work on non-ferrous metals.

WRENCH
　　Any tool for levering or twisting. Particularly useful for turning nuts and bolts.

WROUGHT IRON
　　Iron with little or no carbon. Produced by the puddling process

Z

ZINC
　　Grey/white metal used mainly in alloys and for coating steel

ZINC CHLORIDE
　　Chemical used as a flux for soldering.

Properties of Metals

Metal	Chemical symbol	Pounds per cubic in.	Melting Point Degrees F
Aluminum	Al	0.0924	1218
Cadmium	Cd	0.3105	610
Chromium	Cr	0.2347	2939
Cobolt	Co	0.3123	2696
Copper	Cu	0.3184	1981
Gold	Au	0.6975	1945
Iron (wrought)	Fe	0.2834	2750
Lead	Pb	0.4105	621
Magnesium	Mg	0.0628	1204
Nickel	Ni	0.3177	2646
Silver	Ag	0.3802	1761
Tin	Sn	0.2632	449
Zinc	Zn	0.2587	787

Properties of Alloys

Alloy	Composition	Pounds Per Cubic Inch	Melting Point Degrees F
Brass Or	80 copper, 20 zinc	0.3105	1846
Spelter	60 copper, 40 zinc	0.3018	1634
	50 copper, 50 zinc	0.2960	1616
Solder	20 tin, 80 lead	-	532
	40 tin, 60 lead	-	446
	40 tin, 60 lead	-	446
	50 tin, 50 lead	-	401
	60 tin, 40 lead	-	369
	70 tin, 30 lead	-	365
	90 tin, 10 lead	-	419
Steel	-	0.2816	2500

Soldering Fluxes

Prepared fluxes can be purchased, but the following are traditional fluxes for soft soldering. For hand soldering all suitable metals, use borax.

Metal Or Alloy	Flux
Aluminum	Stearin
Brass	Chloride of zinc or resin
Copper	Chloride of zinc or resin
Lead	Tallow or resin
Tinned steel	Chloride of zinc or resin
Galvanized steel	Hydrochloric acid
Zinc	Hydrochloric acid
Pewter	Gallipoli oil
Iron and steel	Chloride of zinc or chloride of ammonia

Composition of Some Alloys

Alloy	copper	lead	tin	zinc	Antimony
Brass	32	-	1.5	10	-
Gunmetal	80	-	10	-	-
Gilding metal	60	-	-	40	-
Bell metal	80	-	20	-	-
Spelter	50	-	-	50	-
Solder	-	60	40	-	-
Britannia metal	2	-	90	-	8
Pewter	2	2	89	-	7
Type metal	-	50	25	0	25